WORLD OF ANIMALS

45

AMPHIBIANS AND REPTILES

LIZARDS 2

Geckos, Wall Lizards, Whiptails, Racerunners ...

CHRIS MATTISON

GROLIER
an imprint of
SCHOLASTIC
www.scholastic.com/librarypublishing

Representative lizard species: Moorish gecko, Tarentola mauritanica (1); Turkish gecko, Hemidactylus turcicus (2); tegu, Tupinambis teguixin (3).

Published 2005 by Grolier, an imprint of Scholastic Library Publishing Danbury, CT 06816

This edition published exclusively for the school and library market

The Brown Reference Group plc.
(incorporating Andromeda Oxford Limited)
8 Chapel Place
Rivington Street
London
EC2A 3DQ

© 2005 The Brown Reference Group plc.

Library of Congress Cataloging-in-Publication Data

Amphibians and Reptiles.
    p. cm. -- (World of Animals; v. 41-50)
    Contents: [1] Salamanders, newts, and caecilians / Chris Mattison -- [2] Frogs and toads 1 / Chris Mattison -- [3] Frogs and toads 2 / Chris Mattison -- [4] Lizards 1 / Valerie Davies, Chris Mattison -- [5] Lizards 2 / Chris Mattison -- [6] Lizards 3 / Valerie Davies, Chris Mattison -- [7] Turtles and crocodilians / David Alderton -- [8] Snakes 1 / Chris Mattison -- [9] Snakes 2 / Chris Mattison -- [10] Snakes 3 / Chris Mattison.
    ISBN 0-7172-5916-1 (set : alk. paper) -- ISBN 0-7172-5917-X (v. 1 : alk. paper) -- ISBN 0-7172-5918-8 (v. 2 : alk. paper) -- ISBN 0-7172-5919-6 (v. 3 : alk. paper) -- ISBN 0-7172-5920-X (v. 4 : alk. paper) -- ISBN 0-7172-5921-8 (v. 5 : alk. paper) -- ISBN 0-7172-5922-6 (v. 6 : alk. paper) -- ISBN 0-7172-5923-4 (v. 7 : alk. paper) -- ISBN 0-7172-5924-2 (v. 8 : alk. paper) -- ISBN 0-7172-5925-0 (v. 9 : alk. paper) -- ISBN 0-7172-5926-9 (v. 10 : alk. paper)
    1. Amphibians -- Juvenile literature. 2. Reptiles -- Juvenile literature [1. Amphibians. 2. Reptiles.] I. Grolier (Firm) II. Series: World of Animals (Danbury, Conn.); v. 41-50.
QL49.W877 2003
590--dc22   2002073860

Set ISBN 0-7172-5916-1

Project Directors: Graham Bateman, Lindsey Lowe
Editors: Virginia Carter, Angela Davies
Art Editor and Designer: Steve McCurdy
Picture Manager: Becky Cox
Picture Researcher: Alison Floyd
Main Artists: Denys Ovenden, Philip Hood, Myke Taylor, Ken Oliver, Michael Woods, David M. Dennis
Maps: Steve McCurdy, Tim Williams
Production: Alastair Gourlay, Maggie Copeland

Printed in Singapore

About This Volume

This volume deals with nine of the 12 families of lizards. Among the typical geckos there are many species that have adhesive toe pads enabling them to climb smooth surfaces and even to hang upside down. Some of them have found a suitable substitute for their natural habitat in human settlements, using walls as rock faces and hunting the flies, moths, and cockroaches that are attracted by artificial lights. Others live in burrows or rock piles, retreating from the searing heat during the day and emerging after dark to hunt on gravel, rock, or sand. Many geckos are wonderfully camouflaged and seem to disappear when they come to rest on mottled rock or mossy tree bark. A small proportion of species have become active during the day, and some of them are brightly colored.

Other lizards dealt with include the flap-footed lizards and the night lizards. They are small families containing small, secretive species with some similarities to geckos, but whose lives are poorly known. The Old World wall lizards and their relatives are easier to study as they dash about on walls and rock faces or hunt among the gravel and sand of African deserts. There are also tree dwellers and grass lizards among them, and the family is closely paralleled by the American whiptails and racerunners, a widespread and successful family that includes the giant tegus from South America. Finally, the African girdle-tailed and plated lizards are rock lovers, living on sandstone or granite outcrops and basking and foraging within a few yards of deep crevices into which they jam themselves if they are chased by predators.

Contents

The streamlined body shape of the six-lined lizard, Takydromus sexlineatus, *is ideal for sliding through dense undergrowth.*

The western banded gecko, Coleonyx variegatus, *lives in the deserts of the American Southwest and Mexico.*

In the deserts of southern Africa the wedge-snouted sand lizard, Meroles cuneirostris, *is a proficient "sand swimmer."*

How to Use This Set

World of Animals: Amphibians and Reptiles is a 10-volume set that describes in detail reptiles and amphibians from all corners of the earth. Each volume brings together those animals that are most closely related and have similar lifestyles. So all the frogs and toads are in Volumes 42 and 43, the snakes are in Volumes 48, 49, and 50, and so on. To help you find volumes that interest you, look at pages 6 and 7 (Find the Animal). A brief introduction to each volume is also given on page 2 (About This Volume).

Article Styles

Each volume contains two types of article. The first kind introduces major groups (such as amphibians, reptiles, frogs and toads, or lizards). It presents a general overview of the subject.

The second type of article makes up most of each volume. It describes in detail individual species, such as the American bullfrog or the American alligator, or groups of very similar animals, such as reed frogs or day geckos. Each article starts with a fact-filled **data panel** to help you gather information at a glance. Used together, the two different styles of article will enable you to become familiar with animals in the context of their evolutionary history and biological relationships.

Data panel presents basic statistics of each animal

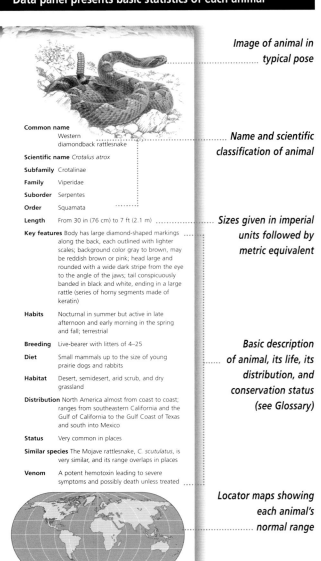

Image of animal in typical pose

Common name
Western diamondback rattlesnake

Name and scientific classification of animal

Scientific name Crotalus atrox

Subfamily Crotalinae

Family Viperidae

Suborder Serpentes

Order Squamata

Length From 30 in (76 cm) to 7 ft (2.1 m)

Sizes given in imperial units followed by metric equivalent

Key features Body has large diamond-shaped markings along the back, each outlined with lighter scales; background color gray to brown, may be reddish brown or pink; head large and rounded with a wide dark stripe from the eye to the angle of the jaws; tail conspicuously banded in black and white, ending in a large rattle (series of horny segments made of keratin)

Habits Nocturnal in summer but active in late afternoon and early morning in the spring and fall; terrestrial

Breeding Live-bearer with litters of 4–25

Diet Small mammals up to the size of young prairie dogs and rabbits

Habitat Desert, semidesert, arid scrub, and dry grassland

Distribution North America almost from coast to coast; ranges from southeastern California and the Gulf of California to the Gulf Coast of Texas and south into Mexico

Status Very common in places

Similar species The Mojave rattlesnake, *C. scutulatus*, is very similar, and its range overlaps in places

Venom A potent hemotoxin leading to severe symptoms and possibly death unless treated

Basic description of animal, its life, its distribution, and conservation status (see Glossary)

Locator maps showing each animal's normal range

Article describes a particular animal

Scientific name of animal

Common name of animal

FROGS AND TOADS

Common European Treefrog
Hyla arborea

The treefrogs commonly seen near water throughout most of continental Europe belong to the Hyla arborea complex of species. They are prolific breeders with loud, raucous calls.

Common name Common European tree frog (green tree frog)

Scientific name Hyla arborea

Subfamily Hylinae

Family Hylidae

Order Anura

Size From 1.25 in (3 cm) to 2 in (5 cm)

Key features Body plump; color usually bright green, although individuals can change color; there is nearly always a dark line running through the eye; dark line continues onto the flanks, an extension of the line projects upward at an angle just above the groin; toes have well-developed pads

Habits Mainly nocturnal but diurnal on humid or rainy days; arboreal

Breeding Throughout the summer in shallow water; female lays clutches of 200–1,400 eggs; eggs hatch after 14–21 days

Diet Insects, especially flies

Habitat Heavily vegetated areas near water, such as reed beds, hedges, bushes, and trees

Distribution Throughout most of Europe except the British Isles, parts of southern France, southern and eastern Iberia; also into Asiatic Turkey and through the former Soviet states as far as the Caspian Sea

Status Very common in places

Similar species There are many closely related species, each occurring where the others do not—their ranges only rarely overlap

THE COMMON EUROPEAN TREEFROG lives in a variety of habitats, sometimes several hundred yards from water. It is most common in reed beds, however, or in bushes and shrubs around the edges of ponds. Juveniles tend to live lower down among the vegetation, and they often occur in large numbers in waist-high vegetation, while the adults—having climbed into higher parts of trees and shrubs—are nowhere to be seen. They hide during the day in hot, dry weather but may bask in an exposed position on days when the air is not too dry. When resting in a exposed position, they often turn bright yellowish green in color.

In Spain and Portugal where the frog's range overlaps that of the stripeless treefrog, Hyla meridionalis, it is often found at higher elevations (presumably because it tolerates lower temperatures), so the two species are not in direct competition. In the Canary Islands the stripeless treefrog tolerates very hot conditions and often occurs in banana plantations, where it breeds in irrigation ditches.

Raucous Choruses
Breeding takes place in shallow ponds that can be quite small. Water temperature is an important factor, and ponds in exposed positions are favored over those with the water's surface bushes. Males call from aquatic vegetation. Their call is loud and raucous. If there are only two or three males calling, they usually synchronize, but once large numbers start up, the choruses soon become haphazard. They often continue

⊕ *The stripeless treefrog, Hyla meridionalis, is similar to the common European treefrog, but as its common name suggests, it lacks the stripe down its side. Its long legs and expanded toe pads give it remarkable agility for climbing and jumping.*

SEE ALSO Treefrogs 43:32; Treefrog, American Green 43:48

46

Cross-references to relevant pages in this and other volumes

Captions to photographs provide additional information about each animal's lifestyle

A number of other features help you navigate through the volumes and present you with helpful extra information. At the bottom of many pages are **cross-references** to other articles of interest. They may be to related animals, animals that live in similar places, or that have similar behavior, predators (or prey), lifestyles, and much more. Each volume also contains a **Set Index** to the complete *World of Animals: Amphibians and Reptiles*. Animals mentioned in the text are indexed by common and scientific names, and many topics are also covered. There is also a **Glossary** that will help you understand certain technical words. Each volume includes lists of useful **Further Reading and Websites** that help you take your research further.

Graphic full-color photographs bring text to life

Easy-to-read and comprehensive text

Tables summarize classification of groups

Who's Who tables summarize classification of each major group

Detailed diagrams illustrate text

Introductory article describes family or closely related groups

SNAKES
Vipers and Pit Vipers

Cross-section of the jaw of a rattlesnake, showing the pterygoid and transpalatine bones that push the maxilla bone (holding the fangs) forward when the snake is ready to strike.

Common name Vipers and Pit Vipers **Family** Viperidae

Typical Vipers

Introductory article describes major groups of animals

Arborea Complex

Egg Clumps

SALAMANDERS

Respiration

Food and Feeding

Temperature and Sex

Reproduction

Who's Who among the Salamanders?

Order Caudata (formerly Urodela)

At-a-glance boxes cover topics of special interest

Meticulous drawings illustrate a typical selection of group members

Find the Animal

World of Animals: Amphibians and Reptiles is the fifth part of a library that describes all groups of living animals. Each cluster of volumes in World of Animals covers a familiar group of animals—mammals, birds, reptiles and amphibians, fish, and insects and other invertebrates.

The Animal Kingdom

The living world is divided into five kingdoms, one of which (kingdom Animalia) is the main subject of the World of Animals. Kingdom Animalia is divided into major groups called phyla. The phylum Chordata contains those animals that have a backbone—mammals, birds, reptiles, amphibians, and fish. Animals without backbones (so-called invertebrates, such as insects, spiders, mollusks, and crustaceans) belong to many different phyla. To find which set of volumes in the World of Animals you need, see the chart below.

World of Animals: Amphibians and Reptiles deals with two of the oldest lineages of land animals—the amphibians, which evolved from fish some 400 million years ago, and the reptiles, which evolved from amphibians about 350 million years ago. Although they are no longer dominant animals on earth (unlike the early reptiles typified by the dinosaurs), over 5,000 amphibian species and 8,000 species of reptiles can still be found. Most live in warmer or tropical regions of the world.

Naming Animals

To discuss animals, names are needed for the different kinds. Western diamondback rattlesnakes are one kind of snake, and sidewinders are another.

Rank	Scientific name	Common name
Kingdom	Animalia	Animals
Phylum	Chordata	Animals with a backbone
Class	Reptilia	Reptiles
Order	Squamata	Lizards, Snakes, Amphisbaenians
Suborder	Serpentes	Snakes
Family	Viperidae	Vipers and Pit Vipers
Genus	Crotalus	Rattlesnakes
Species	Crotalus atrox	Western diamondback rattlesnake

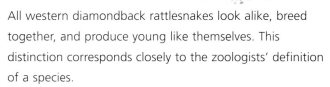

The kingdom Animalia is subdivided into phyla, classes, orders, families, genera, and species. Above is the classification for the western diamondback rattlesnake.

All western diamondback rattlesnakes look alike, breed together, and produce young like themselves. This distinction corresponds closely to the zoologists' definition of a species.

Zoologists use an internationally recognized system for naming species consisting of two-word scientific names, usually in Latin or Greek. The western diamondback rattlesnake is called *Crotalus atrox,* and the sidewinder *Crotalus cerastes. Crotalus* is the name of the genus (a group of very similar species); *atrox* or *cerastes* indicates the species in the genus. The same scientific names are recognized the world over. However, a species

⊕ *This chart lists the phyla in two of the five kingdoms. The phylum Arthropoda makes up a high proportion of all invertebrate animals.*

⊕ *The main groups of animals alive today. Volumes that cover each major group are indicated below.*

ANIMALS Kingdom Animalia		**SINGLE-CELLED LIFE** Kingdom Protista

Vertebrates/ Chordates Phylum Chordata		**Invertebrates** Numerous Phyla

Mammals Class Mammalia	**Birds** Class Aves	**Reptiles** Class Reptilia	**Amphibians** Class Amphibia	**Fish** Several classes	**Insects, spiders, mollusks, spiny-skinned animals, worms**	**Single-Celled Life**
Volumes 1–10	*Volumes 11–20*	*Volumes 44–50*	*Volumes 41–43*	*Volumes 31–40*	*Volumes 21–30*	*Volume 21 (part)*

Groups of Amphibians and Reptiles

CLASS: AMPHIBIA—AMPHIBIANS

ORDER: Gymnophiona (Vol. 41)	caecilians
ORDER: Caudata (Vol. 41)	salamanders and newts
ORDER: Anura (Vols. 42–43)	frogs and toads
Family: Ascaphidae (Vol. 42)	tailed frogs
Family: Leiopelmatidae (Vol. 42)	New Zealand frogs
Family: Bombinatoridae (Vol. 42)	fire-bellied toads
Family: Discoglossidae (Vol. 42)	painted frogs and midwife toads
Family: Megophryidae (Vol. 42)	Asian horned toads and litter frogs
Family: Pelobatidae (Vol. 42)	spadefoot toads
Family: Pelodytidae (Vol. 42)	parsley frogs
Family: Pipidae (Vol. 42)	clawed and Surinam toads
Family: Rhinophrynidae (Vol. 42)	Mexican burrowing frogs
Family: Heleophrynidae (Vol. 43)	ghost frogs
Family: Myobatrachidae (Vol. 42)	southern frogs and Australian toadlets
Family: Sooglossidae (Vol. 43)	Seychelles frogs
Family: Leptodactylidae (Vol. 42)	rain frogs
Family: Bufonidae (Vol. 42)	true toads and harlequin toads
Family: Brachycephalidae (Vol. 42)	three-toed toadlets
Family: Dendrobatidae (Vol. 43)	poison dart frogs
Family: Rhinodermatidae (Vol. 43)	gastric-brooding frogs
Family: Hylidae (Vol.43)	treefrogs, marsupial frogs, and leaf frogs
Family: Pseudidae (Vol. 43)	paradoxical frogs
Family: Centrolenidae (Vol. 43)	glass frogs
Family: Allophrynidae (Vol. 43)	no common name
Family: Ranidae (Vol. 43)	water frogs
Family: Arthroleptidae (Vol. 43)	bush squeakers
Family: Hemisotidae (Vol. 43)	shovel-nosed frogs
Family: Hyperoliidae (Vol. 43)	reed frogs and relatives
Family: Rhacophoridae (Vol. 43)	Afro-Asian treefrogs
Family: Mantellidae (Vol. 43)	Madagascan frogs
Family: Microhylidae (Vol. 42)	narrow-mouthed frogs

CLASS: REPTILIA—REPTILES

ORDER: Squamata—lizards, snakes, and amphisbaenians	
Suborder: Sauria (Vols. 44–46)	lizards
Family: Agamidae (Vol. 44)	agamas and dragon lizards
Family: Chamaeleonidae (Vol. 44)	chameleons and dwarf chameleons
Family: Iguanidae (Vol. 44)	iguanas, basilisks, collared lizards, and anoles

Family: Gekkonidae (Vol. 45)	"typical" geckos
Family: Diplodactylidae (Vol. 45)	southern geckos
Family: Pygopodidae (Vol. 45)	flap-footed lizards
Family: Eublepharidae (Vol. 45)	eyelid geckos
Family: Teiidae (Vol. 45)	tegus, whiptails, and racerunners
Family: Gymnophthalmidae (Vol. 45)	spectacled lizards
Family: Lacertidae (Vol. 45)	wall lizards
Family: Xantusiidae (Vol. 45)	night lizards
Family: Scincidae (Vol. 46)	skinks
Family: Gerrhosauridae (Vol. 45)	plated lizards
Family: Cordylidae (Vol. 45)	girdle-tailed lizards
Family: Dibamidae (Vol. 45)	blind lizards
Family: Xenosauridae (Vol. 46)	knob-scaled and crocodile lizards
Family: Anguidae (Vol. 46)	alligator and glass lizards
Family: Varanidae (Vol. 46)	monitor lizards
Family: Helodermatidae (Vol. 46)	beaded lizards
Family: Lanthonotidae (Vol. 46)	Borneo earless monitor
Suborder: Amphisbaenia (Vol. 46)	amphisbaenians (worm lizards)
Suborder: Serpentes (Vols. 48–50)	snakes
Family: Anomalepidae (Vol. 48)	dawn blind snakes
Family: Leptotyphlopidae (Vol. 48)	thread snakes
Family: Typhlopidae (Vol. 48)	blind snakes
Family: Anomochilidae (Vol. 48)	dwarf pipe snakes
Family: Uropeltidae (Vol. 48)	shield-tailed snakes
Family: Cylindrophiidae (Vol. 48)	pipe snakes
Family: Aniliidae (Vol. 48)	South American pipe snake
Family: Xenopeltidae (Vol. 48)	Asian sunbeam snakes
Family: Loxocemidae (Vol. 48)	American sunbeam snake
Family: Acrochordidae (Vol. 48)	file snakes
Family: Boidae (Vol. 48)	boas
Family: Bolyeriidae (Vol. 48)	Round Island boas
Family: Tropidophiidae (Vol. 48)	wood snakes
Family: Pythonidae (Vol. 48)	pythons
Family: Colubridae (Vol. 49)	colubrids
Family: Atractaspididae (Vol. 49)	African burrowing snakes
Family: Elapidae (Vol. 50)	cobras
Family: Viperidae (Vol. 50)	vipers and pit vipers
ORDER: Testudines (Vol. 47)	turtles, terrapins, and tortoises
ORDER: Crocodylia (Vol. 47)	crocodiles, alligators, and caimans
ORDER: Rhynchocephalia (Vol. 44)	tuataras

may have been described and named at different times without the zoologists realizing it was one species.

Classification allows us to make statements about larger groups of animals. For example, all rattlesnakes are vipers—along with other vipers they are placed in the family Viperidae. All vipers are placed with all other snakes in the suborder Serpentes; snakes are related to lizards, which are in the suborder Sauria, and so these two groups combine to form the order Squamata in the class Reptilia.

An important point must be made about the current scientific knowledge of these animals. New discoveries are being made every day, from the biology of individual creatures to the finding and naming of new species. Our knowledge of the relationships among the different groups is changing constantly. In addition, the number of species known increases all the time, particularly in the light of the very latest DNA analysis techniques that are available to zoologists.

Geckos

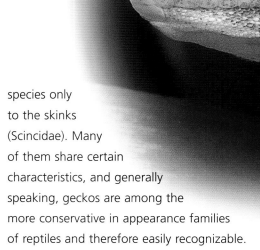

All geckos used to be classified as a single family, the Gekkonidae, but scientists now recognize at least three families: The Gekkonidae contains the "typical" geckos; the Eublepharidae, the eyelid geckos; and the Diplodactylidae, the so-called "southern geckos." A fourth family, the flap-footed lizards (Pygopodidae) is closely related to the geckos and is also included here, as is the Dibamidae, a family of very uncertain relationships.

The Gekkonidae

The most numerous family is the Gekkonidae. With about 910 species in 75 genera it ranks second in number of

Common name Geckos **Order** Squamata

The geckos are divided into three families. Two other families, the Pygopodidae (flap-footed lizards) and the Dibamidae (blind lizards), are allied to them.

Family Gekkonidae—75 genera, about 910 species of typical geckos and American dwarf geckos, sometimes divided into 2 subfamilies
  Subfamily Gekkoninae—about 70 genera, 770 species of typical geckos, including the tokay, *Gekko gecko*, the Moorish gecko, *Tarentola mauretanica*, and the day geckos, *Phelsuma* sp.
  Subfamily Sphaerodactylinae—5 genera, 140 species of American dwarf geckos, including the ashy gecko, *Sphaerodactylus elegans*, and the striped day gecko, *Gonatodes vittatus*

Family Eublepharidae—6 genera, 22 species of eyelid geckos
  Subfamily Aleuroscalobotinae—1 species, the cat gecko, *Aleuroscalobotes felinus* from Southeast Asia
  Subfamily Eublepharinae—5 genera, 21 species with a global distribution, including the western banded gecko, *Coleonyx variegatus*, and the leopard gecko, *Eublepharis macularius*

Family Diplodactylidae—14 genera, about 115 species of "southern" geckos, including the Australian leaf-tailed geckos, *Saltuarius* sp., the golden-tailed gecko, *Diplodactylus taenicauda*, and the live-bearing gecko, *Rhacodactylus trachyrhynchus* from New Caledonia

Family Pygopodidae—7 genera, 35 species of flap-footed lizards from Australia and southern New Guinea in 2 subfamilies
  Subfamily Pygopodinae—3 genera, 20 species, including the black-headed scaly-foot, *Pygopus nigriceps*
  Subfamily Lialisinae—4 genera, 15 species, including Burton's snake lizard, *Lialis burtoni*

Family Dibamidae—2 genera, 10 species of poorly studied "blind" lizards from Southeast Asia and Mexico

species only to the skinks (Scincidae). Many of them share certain characteristics, and generally speaking, geckos are among the more conservative in appearance families of reptiles and therefore easily recognizable.

Gekkonid, or "typical," geckos have no eyelids. The eyelids have become fused and transparent (like those of snakes) and are shed along with the rest of the skin. Most species are nocturnal, so their eyes are large, and they often use their tongues to wipe them clean. In bright light the pupils of the eyes of nocturnal species close down to vertical slits with a number of small pinhole openings. Their irises are often intricately marked and can be quite beautiful. Diurnal species, which include all the small species in the subfamily Sphaerodactylinae, members of *Phelsuma* in the subfamily Gekkoninae, and several other genera as well, account for perhaps one-tenth of all geckos. They have smaller eyes and round pupils.

Typical geckos have an almost worldwide distribution and are absent only from the Arctic and Antarctic regions. They are successful colonizers of islands and archipelagos throughout the world's oceans and may be the only lizards present on some of the smaller ones. A tendency to wander has also resulted in the accidental introduction of many species to places where they are not native. Some species are so closely allied to man-made habitats that they are rarely found anywhere else.

Members of the Gekkonidae range in size from tiny creatures such as the American *Sphaerodactylus* species,

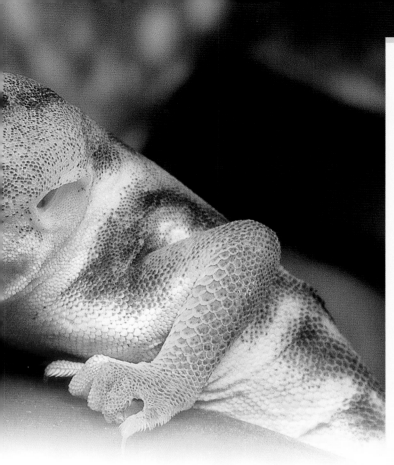

↑ **The frog-eyed gecko,** Teratoscincus microlepis *from Asia, belongs to the family Gekkonidae. It is unusual among gekkonids in having large overlapping scales.*

at about 2 inches (5 cm) long, to the giant gecko from New Caledonia, *Rhacodactylus leachianus,* which grows to 13 inches (33 cm) from its snout to the end of its body. Its tail is short and stubby, and adds only a couple more inches to the total length. A more common species, the large, pugnacious tokay, *Gekko gecko,* grows to just over 13 inches (33 cm) in total.

Subdued Appearance

Nearly all gekkonids have small granular scales, but some also have larger tubercular scales scattered among the small ones. A few species, notably the ground-dwelling frog-eyed geckos in the genus *Teratoscincus* (six species from Asia) and the fish-scale geckos, *Geckolepis* (five species from Madagascar), have larger overlapping scales.

Nocturnal geckos tend to be dull in color, often gray or brown with indistinct, mottled markings. Many have a limited ability to change shade, becoming paler at night. The tokay is an exception: It is gray-blue in color with

How Do They Stick and Move?

Geckos are spectacular climbers, but establishing exactly how their toes stick has not been straightforward. Unlike treefrogs, geckos do not grip by suction—if they did, they would be able to stick to wet surfaces, which they cannot. Nor do they have minute hairs on their feet ending in tiny hooks for gripping small irregularities in surfaces—if they did, a piece of perfectly clean glass would defeat them, and it does not. In fact, the smoother the surface, the better they stick. It now seems likely that they use "surface energy," or "surface adhesion." This force is the same one that creates surface tension on water, for instance, which is the reason why a pond skater can live on the water's surface without sinking.

The physics of this phenomenon are complex, but experiments have shown that the gecko relies on the molecular attraction across closely positioned surfaces. The gecko's toe pads are made up of special structures called lamellae that form rows across each toe pad. Each lamella consists of thousands of hairlike cells known as setae, and each seta is again divided into even smaller branches. Each of the branches ends in a slightly swollen, or spatulate, structure, of which there can be up to one billion altogether. Their cumulative surface energy is more than enough to support the gecko.

With all these setae acting together to allow the gecko to cling to a smooth surface, it could easily become stuck. It gets around this problem by curling up the ends of its toes when it wants to move its foot—in effect "unpeeling'" them from the surface. Of course, all this happens so quickly that it is usually impossible to follow with the human eye.

Geckos are nature's supreme climbers thanks to the enlarged adhesive toe pads containing thousands of microscopic setae.

spots of orange or blood-red covering its entire body. Diurnal geckos are often colorful, the most attractive being the day geckos, *Phelsuma* from Madagascar and other islands in the Indian Ocean. Most are bright green with red markings, while some are bluish-green or

Versatile Tails

Geckos are often prone to discarding their tails if they are grasped: Finding an individual that does not have a regrown tail is almost impossible in some populations, although species that use their tails to store fat or that have very short, stumplike tails are less inclined to sacrifice them.

There is more to a gecko's tail than this, however. Many species, such as several naked-toed geckos, *Cyrtodactylus* species from Asia, the leopard gecko, *Eublepharis macularius*, and the Australian velvet geckos, *Oedura* species, have tails that are banded in black and white. They serve to distract predators, which then attack the tail rather than a more vulnerable part of the gecko's body. Many species, especially those from arid regions, have thick, carrot-shaped tails that are used to store food. A few, notably the Madagascan and Australian leaf-tailed geckos, *Uroplatus* and *Phyllurus* respectively, have tails that are flattened and leaflike. These geckos press them against the tree trunks on which they rest to eliminate shadows. The Asian flying, or parachute, geckos, *Ptychozoon*, have a scalloped fringe running around the edge of the tail that increases air resistance and helps them glide.

Other activities associated with geckos' tails include the production of sound or substances. The wonder geckos, *Teratoscincus* species, and the viper gecko, *Teratolepis fasciata*, produce a sound by moving their tail and thereby rubbing together the large scales covering it, a process known as stridulation (which is more common in insects such as crickets and grasshoppers). Some *Diplodactylus* species produce a sticky substance in glands in the tail; if they are in danger, they deter predators by spraying them with it. Staying in Australia, the knob-tailed geckos, *Nephrurus* species, have small knobs on the end of the tail that are well endowed with nerve endings. Scientists believe that they may be important in chemical communication, thermoregulation, or defense.

turquoise. Some of the dwarf geckos, *Lygodactylus* species from Africa, are also colorful with yellow or black-and-white heads.

Sticky Toe Pads

A number of different species are known as "house" geckos. One of their more notable characteristics is the presence of adhesive pads at the ends of their toes. They vary slightly in shape but have expanded surfaces that enable the geckos to run up any type of vertical surface, rough or smooth, and even to rest upside down on ceilings. The exact design of the toes and their pads varies from genus to genus, and the scientific names often reflect this. So we have, for instance, *Hemidactylus*, meaning "half toe," *Sphaerodactylus*, meaning "ball toe," and *Phyllodactylus*, meaning "leaflike toe."

Other species do not have adhesive pads, however. They are divided into the ground geckos that do not climb at all, such as *Chondrodactylus* ("grain toe") and *Pachydactylus* ("thick toe"), and the species that climb into trees and bushes and use claws rather than pads. They include members of the genera *Cyrtodactylus* ("curved toe") and *Gymnodactylus* ("naked toe").

Ground-dwelling geckos are especially common in deserts (where there is often nothing

⊖ *Displaying a brightly colored tail, as in the Thai bow-fingered gecko,* Cyrtodactylus peguensis, *can be a ruse to divert attention away from more vulnerable areas of the body.*

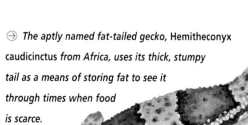

⊖ *The aptly named fat-tailed gecko,* Hemitheconyx caudicinctus *from Africa, uses its thick, stumpy tail as a means of storing fat to see it through times when food is scarce.*

for them to climb anyway), and they typically live in burrows or rock crevices. Many have plump tails in which they store fat, and some have large heads with powerful jaws for crushing hard-bodied insects such as beetles. In Africa two species of web-footed geckos in the genus *Palmatogecko* have webbed feet to help them run across loose sand without sinking. Barking geckos, *Ptenopus* species from Africa, have fringes of hairlike scales around the edges of their feet for the same reason. All ground geckos are nocturnal.

Of the two subfamilies the Gekkoninae contains all the medium to large species from the Old World, such as the tokay, *Gekko gecko,* the day geckos, *Phelsuma* species, and the house geckos, *Hemidactylus* species and others, as well as some from the New World, such as the turnip-tailed gecko, *Thecadactylus rapicauda.* All members of this subfamily lay hard-shelled eggs, usually in pairs but occasionally singly or in threes. The small, diurnal sphaerodactyline geckos are restricted to the New World, mainly to Central and South America. In many species males are more brightly colored than females. In the striped gecko, *Gonatodes vittatus* from northern South America, their color varies so much that the two sexes look as though they belong to different species. These tiny geckos also lay hard-shelled eggs, but the clutches consist of a single egg.

The Diplodactylidae

The Diplodactylidae are sometimes known as "southern" geckos because they are found only in Australia, New Zealand, and New Caledonia. There are about 115 species in 14 genera, and they include several unusual species. Southern geckos produce two offspring, like most typical geckos, but they may either lay soft-shelled eggs or give

⊖ *Six species of giant geckos in the genus* Rhacodactylus *are endemic to New Caledonia.* Rhacodactylus ciliatus *has a row of enlarged, spinelike scales above the eye and along the neck.*

birth to live young. The New Zealand geckos belonging to the genera *Hoplodactylus* and *Naultinus,* with 10 and eight species respectively, are all live-bearers, as is a single species from New Caledonia, *Rhacodactylus trachyrhynchus.* Five other species of *Rhacodactylus* (all from New Caledonia) are egg layers.

Live-bearing species often have long gestation periods: The spotted sticky-toed gecko, *Hoplodactylus maculatus,* has a 14–month pregnancy and therefore only breeds every second year. Even so, it only gives birth to two young. It therefore has the lowest reproductive potential of any lizard, indicating that its life span is long.

Australian species include the leaf-tailed geckos, *Phyllurus,* and nine species of knob-tailed geckos, *Nephrurus.* As their common name suggests, their tails (which are very short in some species) end in a small knob that is well equipped with nerve endings and may be used in communication or thermoregulation.

Southern geckos live in a variety of habitats. Many are desert dwellers, while others are arboreal. They include many of the velvet geckos, *Oedura*, which are often habitat specific—some live under the bark of fallen trees, others inhabit standing trees, and yet others make their home under flakes of rocks.

The fringe-toed velvet gecko, *Oedura filicipoda*, has a fringe of scales around its toes to enhance its climbing abilities. It has a prehensile tail that helps it clamber about in vegetation. The same tail adaptation is also found in the jeweled gecko, *Diplodactylus elderi* from Australia, and the New Zealand day geckos, *Naultinus* species, as well as three species of *Eurydactylodes* from New Caledonia. In addition, the fringe-toed gecko, the New Caledonian geckos, *Rhacodactylus*, and the pad-tailed gecko, *Pseudothecadactylus australis*, have adhesive pads on the tips of their prehensile tails to supplement those found on their toes.

12 **SEE ALSO** Gecko, Giant Leaf-Tailed **45**:20; Gecko, Moorish **45**:28; Lizards, Flap-Footed **45**:48; Worm Lizards **46**:102

The Eublepharidae

The Eublepharidae is the most primitive of the gecko families. All of its members have movable eyelids—they are often referred to as the eyelid geckos—and none of them have sticky toe pads. They are all ground dwellers except for the cat gecko, *Aleuroscalabotes felinus* from Malaysia. This unusual species is semiarboreal and has a prehensile tail that it holds in a coiled position as it moves slowly along twigs.

Other eyelid geckos live in North and Central America (*Coleonyx* species), in Africa (*Hemitheconyx* and *Holodactylus* species), in the Middle East (*Eublepharis*), and in Japan and eastern China (*Goniurosaurus*). There are 22 species altogether, and their scattered distribution indicates that they were once more widespread. The species that remain are relicts of a much larger family that had an extensive range.

Eyelid geckos lay their eggs in pairs (but occasionally singly or in threes). Like the southern geckos, they have a pliable shell that absorbs water during its development. Species from North America, Africa, and the Middle East live in dry habitats, those from Central America and Asia live in rain forests, while the species from Japan and China live in cool, moist habitats, especially caves. One characteristic of the species that have been studied to date is that they defecate in one place, as though marking a territory.

The Dibamidae

The biology of this family of "blind" lizards is practically unknown. It contains 10 species, of which nine are in the genus *Dibamus*, living in the forests of Southeast Asia; the other species, *Anelytropsis papillosus*, lives in Mexico. All are limbless, although the males have small vestigial (reduced) hind limbs in the form of scaly flaps like those of some of the Australian flap-footed lizards. Their eyes are also vestigial and are covered by a single scale, and they have no external ear openings. They burrow in soil or live in or under rotting logs and grow to a maximum of about 10 inches (25 cm) including their tails. Nothing is known about their eating habits or breeding behavior, although females of the species studied so far lay clutches consisting of a single egg.

Scientists are undecided on where blind lizards come in the scheme of things, and some believe them to be more closely related to the worm lizards (suborder Amphisbaenia) than to the true lizards in the suborder Sauria.

Geckos on Islands

There are few islands where geckos of some sort do not live; on some islands they are the only reptiles. Many of the islands have never been attached to the mainland, so the geckos must have arrived by sea—clinging to drifting debris torn up during a storm on the mainland or possibly as eggs hidden behind the bark of a tree trunk. Geckos are suited to spreading in this way because their eggs are well protected against desiccation. They can survive long journeys before hatching out sometime after reaching their destination. In addition, they often use communal egg-laying sites, with several females laying in the same place. A single landfall can therefore provide enough individuals for a colony to get started. A number of species, including several island species, are parthenogenetic (meaning they are all-female species that can reproduce without males); this is obviously an advantage, since it takes just a single individual to start a colony.

Many island species are widespread. The common house gecko, *Hemidactylus frenatus*, for example, is found throughout the tropical and subtropical world. Others, however, obviously arrived tens of thousands of years earlier and evolved into new forms that were not found anywhere else. On the island of Socotra off the Arabian Peninsula, for instance, there are 18 species of geckos, of which 15 are endemic.

Common name Leopard gecko

Scientific name *Eublepharis macularius*

Subfamily Eublepharinae

Family Eublepharidae

Suborder Sauria

Order Squamata

Size 8 in (20 cm) to 10 in (25 cm) long

Key features This species has eyelids; head broad; body
cylindrical; tail is thick and carrot shaped
when animal is well fed; skin covered with
small tubercles; toes lack adhesive pads; color
yellow or tan with many small, dark-brown
spots over the top of the head, back, and tail,
sometimes with bluish background; spots on
tail superimposed on wide black-and-white
bands; juveniles are completely different with
wide, saddle-shaped, dark-brown markings
on a white or cream background

Habits Terrestrial and nocturnal; seeks refuge from
the heat by day and from the cold in winter
by living in underground burrows

Breeding Female lays 2 soft-shelled eggs; eggs hatch
after 40–60 days

Diet Invertebrates, including insects, spiders, and
scorpions; also other lizards

Habitat Desert and scrub regions in mountainous
areas

Distribution South-central Asia (Pakistan, northwest
India, Iraq, Iran, and Afghanistan)

Status Common

Similar species Other poorly known species of
Eublepharis occur in the region and are
similar to the leopard gecko

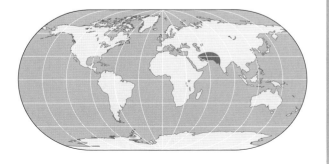

Leopard Gecko

*Eublepharis
macularius*

*Leopard geckos were the first lizard species to be
bred in large numbers for the pet trade. They still
rank among the most popular because they
are tough, attractive, and adapt well to
an artificial environment.*

THE LEOPARD GECKO IS A FAMILIAR REPTILE "pet" that
is kept by the thousands by amateur enthusiasts
and selectively bred to create a number of
attractive color forms. The same qualities that
make it a good pet also make it ideal as a
laboratory animal. Most of the research on
temperature-dependent sex determination
(TDSD) was carried out on the leopard gecko,
leading scientists to look more carefully at this
process in other reptiles. The research has had
important implications for conservation by
means of captive-breeding programs in other
species, especially tortoises and sea turtles.

The natural environment of leopard geckos
is the arid plains and foothills in southern Asia
and the Middle East, where they live among
rock outcrops and desert scrub. They avoid
loose, sandy surfaces. They survive this harsh
environment by being strictly nocturnal and
limiting their period of activity to times when
temperatures are suitable. Because the desert
cools rapidly, leopard geckos are most likely to
be seen on the surface in the hours between
sunset and midnight. After that they retreat
into deep burrows to avoid the extremes of
temperature. During winter they stop coming
out of their tunnels altogether, and they live off
the fat stored in their carrot-shaped tail. The tail
will wither dramatically if the leopard gecko
goes through a long period with no food.

Stiff Legs

Leopard geckos never climb and lack the
adhesive pads on the tips of the toes that some
other geckos have. Instead of pads they have
small claws. Like most other members of the
Eublepharidae (but in contrast to most other

geckos), leopard geckos walk on stiff legs with their body held clear of the ground. They feed mainly on a variety of insects, spiders, and scorpions, and will also eat smaller lizards.

Leopard geckos appear to live in loose colonies centered around a rocky outcrop or a stony hillside. Several females and juveniles may live within a male's territory, but males do not tolerate each other. Leopard geckos lick each other's skin to determine sex, presumably picking up molecules that help with identification.

Breeding takes place in the spring, and females may lay several clutches of two soft-shelled eggs at intervals of a few weeks. They bury the eggs in moist sandy soil, carefully replacing the soil after laying and smoothing it over to disguise the eggs' whereabouts. The eggs usually hatch after between 40 and 60 days depending on the temperature. The sex of the resulting offspring also depends on the incubation temperature.

Sex Determination and Temperature

The sex of the vast majority of lizards and other animals, including humans, is determined genetically by sex chromosomes (in humans XX produces females and XY produces males, for instance). The sex is fixed at the moment of fertilization and depends entirely on which type of spermatozoa (male gamete) reaches the ovum first.

However, a select number of reptiles, including the leopard gecko, use a method known as temperature-dependent sex determination (TDSD), in which the sex of the offspring is not fixed at the time of fertilization nor even when the egg is laid. It changes during the incubation period depending on the temperature. It appears that there is a "time window" during the early part of incubation when the sex can swing one way or another.

In leopard geckos lower temperatures of about 68 to 73°F (20–23°C) produce females and so do high temperatures in the range of 90 to 104°F (32–40°C). Temperatures of about 77 to 86°F (25–30°C) produce mostly males, and temperatures between each of these ranges produce a mix of both sexes.

⊖ *Leopard geckos get their name from the spots covering their body. Juveniles are banded and boldly colored, and appear quite different. The banding and color intensity gradually fade as the gecko matures.*

Leopard Geckos as Pets

It is generally agreed among hobbyists that the leopard gecko is one of the best species of lizards for beginners to keep for several reasons. First, they are tough and undemanding in captivity and will thrive under a variety of conditions. Because they are nocturnal, they do not need ultraviolet light in which to bask. Second, they are calm and unhurried in their movements and less likely to escape than many other species, and they rarely bite. Most importantly, they can be bred in large numbers for distribution through the pet trade.

Many breeders have developed strains with particular color characteristics, some of which have fanciful names, such as "high yellow," "lavender," "striped," "jungle," and "albino." However, all these mutated varieties are equally easy to care for. Although females only lay clutches of two eggs, they will lay every two or three weeks over a long period in the spring and summer. The young are easily reared and reach maturity in one to two years.

A single adult male or a small group of juveniles or females can be kept in a medium-sized aquarium with a layer of paper, bark chippings, or small pebbles. They will always defecate in the same place, so they are easy to keep clean. Temperature is not critical but should be between 73 and 86°F (23–30°C) during the day. A drop of 9 to 18°F (5–10°C) at night will not cause any problems and may be beneficial. The best form of heating is an under-cage heat mat. Placing it at one end of the cage gives the gecko(s) a choice of temperatures. A hiding place should be provided at each end of the cage—the best design for this is an upturned flowerpot or plastic food container with a "door" cut out. The substrate inside the hide should be sprayed to provide a small area of high humidity that will help the gecko shed its skin properly when the time comes.

Leopard geckos can be fed crickets, mealworms, or wax worms from pet suppliers. Spiders and insects can be collected, but only if they come from places that have not been sprayed with chemicals. Too many waxworms can lead to the geckos becoming obese. They should be fed every day, preferably in the evening, although geckos in good condition (those with a plump tail) can easily go for two or three days without food. Large numbers of crickets should not be put in the cage if the carer is going away for a few days, since they can cause stress and damage to the geckos. If only cultured food, such as crickets and mealworms, is being used, each meal should be dusted with a calcium or vitamin-and-calcium preparation specially formulated for reptiles. They are available in specialized pet stores. Geckos fed on a variety of wild-collected food do not need any supplements.

⊕ *Research on temperature-dependent sex determination in leopard geckos has helped halt the decline of some endangered species by skewing the sex ratio toward more breeding females.*

Juvenile leopard geckos such as this one lack spots; instead, they are boldly marked with yellow, white, and dark-brown bands. Even when fully grown, leopard geckos only reach about 10 inches (25 cm) long, and their gentle temperament makes them ideal pets.

Some other lizard species and (as far as we know) all crocodilians have a system similar to that of the leopard geckos. But while other reptiles have TDSD, the details can differ. In many turtles, for example, low temperatures produce males, and high ones produce females. In some lizards the situation is the mirror image of this, with high temperatures producing males; while crocodilians and many other lizards follow a system similar to that of the leopard geckos.

Nobody knows how or why this system has evolved, although several theories have been put forward. But the implications for the future of some of these species are more obvious. If global warming continues, the sex ratios of many species could be affected, with a preponderance of males or females depending on which system they are locked into. On a smaller scale deforestation may remove shade from favored egg-laying sites, causing the overall temperature to rise, whereas other circumstances may cause temperatures to fall locally. We have no idea whether or not female geckos (or turtles or crocodilians) can assess the temperature of their egg-laying sites and act accordingly by repositioning their nests to counteract the changes. In all probability they cannot.

On the other hand, the implications for captive-breeding programs are more positive. By manipulating the temperature of the eggs, breeders can decide whether to produce mainly males or females. In some cases an abundance of females will be more useful than males. Before TDSD was properly understood, however, captive-breeding programs, including those in which wild turtle eggs were collected and incubated under controlled conditions, may have fallen foul of TDSD, producing offspring of only one sex.

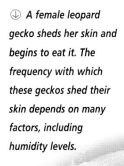

⊕ *A female leopard gecko sheds her skin and begins to eat it. The frequency with which these geckos shed their skin depends on many factors, including humidity levels.*

Common name Western banded gecko

Scientific name *Coleonyx variegatus*

Subfamily Eublepharinae

Family Eublepharidae

Suborder Sauria

Order Squamata

Size From 3.3 in (8 cm) to 4.3 in (12 cm)

Key features A delicate-looking gecko with thin, translucent skin and tiny scales; eyes are large and have functional eyelids; limbs long and thin; toes end in small claws; color variable but usually cream, buff, or yellow with dark-brown crossbands; tail has black-and-white bands

Habits Terrestrial; strictly nocturnal

Breeding Female lays 2 soft-shelled eggs; eggs hatch after about 45 days

Diet Insects, spiders, and small scorpions

Habitat Rocky deserts

Distribution Southwestern United Sates and northwestern Mexico, including Baja California

Status Common

Similar species There are 6 other members of the genus, but a combination of range, size, and markings makes it unlikely that they would be confused with the western banded gecko (or each other)

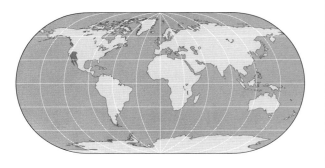

Western Banded Gecko

Coleonyx variegatus

The delicate appearance of the western banded gecko makes it seem an unlikely inhabitant of the hot, dry, environment in which it lives.

THE WESTERN BANDED GECKO'S HABITAT is one of the harshest environments in North America: the rock piles, cacti, and agaves of the American Southwest and adjacent parts of Mexico. Scientists think that the banded geckos, *Coleonyx* species, spread over the region long ago, when conditions were wetter and more humid, and the vegetation was lush.

As the region dried out gradually, the western banded gecko and some of the others adapted to a more arid environment by developing skin that did not lose water as quickly and by limiting themselves to being

Banded Geckos and Superstitions

There are six other members of the genus *Coleonyx*. Two of them, the Texas banded gecko, *C. brevis,* and the Big Bend banded gecko, *C. reticulatus*, live in the southern United States and northern Mexico, but their ranges do not overlap that of the western species. The barefoot gecko, *C. switaki*, lives in southern California and Baja California but is larger than the western banded gecko and not easily confused with it. Two species, *C. elegans* and *C. mitratus*, are restricted to Central America. The remaining species, the black banded gecko, *C. fasciatus* from northwestern Mexico, is very similar in appearance to the western banded gecko, and some scientists consider it to be a subspecies. There is a possible eighth species, *C. gypsicolus* from Isla San Marcos in the Gulf of California. It is very similar in appearance to the barefoot gecko.

People living in Baja California are very afraid of banded geckos of all species, and several superstitions are associated with them. For example, they think that if a gecko walks across your skin, the skin will slough away. Seri Indians believe that the gecko will cause a fatal lung disease if touched and that touching a gecko will cause the flesh to fall off your hands and body.

active on cool nights. In spring before the ground heats up too much, they often shelter closer to the surface during the day under rocks and among the litter of dead agave leaves and cactus pads. But during summer days, when temperatures can rise to lethal levels, they retreat deep underground in burrows and crevices. Two related species, the Yucatán banded gecko, *Coleonyx elegans*, and the Central American banded gecko, *C. mitratus,* live farther south in habitats that are thought to be similar to those in which the ancestral banded geckos lived.

Western banded geckos are often seen wandering around on desert roads at night, usually in the two or three hours before midnight. From a car they look like little white moving twigs or cigarette ends and are easily overlooked if you are traveling at speed. Closer inspection reveals that they walk with their tail curled over their back, and in dim light they can

look like scorpions. They may do this to mimic scorpions in order to deter predators, or it may be a way of deflecting attack away from their head. It may be both, of course.

Juveniles' tails are more boldly banded than those of the adults, and all banded geckos are liable to discard their tails if they are grasped.

Social Interaction

Western banded geckos live in small colonies. Males are highly territorial, and dominant males drive off strange males but tolerate juveniles and females. Breeding starts in early spring, and the females usually begin to lay eggs in May, but this varies slightly according to locality. They lay clutches of two (occasionally one or three) soft-shelled eggs. They bury them in damp sand or soil, usually under a rock or among the roots of a plant. Each female can produce up to three clutches in a single breeding season.

↑ *The fragile-looking western banded gecko has several ways of defending itself. It curls its tail over the back to resemble a scorpion, and its tail can break off easily. The gecko can also make a high-pitched squeak.*

Common name Giant
leaf-tailed gecko

Scientific name *Uroplatus fimbriatus*

Subfamily Gekkoninae

Family Gekkonidae

Suborder Sauria

Order Squamata

Size Up to 12 in (30 cm) long and therefore one
of the largest geckos in the world

Key features Body large and flattened; head large and
triangular; eyes cream in color, massive and
bulging with intricate markings; tail flattened
and leaflike; toes have expanded pads for
climbing and clinging; a frill of skin present
around the lower jaw and along the flanks;
coloration plain or mottled gray or brown,
but it can change from light to dark possibly
in response to temperature

Habits Strictly arboreal and nocturnal

Breeding Female lays 2 hard-shelled eggs; eggs hatch
after about 77–84 days

Diet Invertebrates and possibly smaller lizards

Habitat Rain forests

Distribution Eastern Madagascar

Status Common in suitable habitat but hard to find

Similar species *Uroplatus henkeli* is very similar but has a
more strongly patterned back, is slightly
smaller, and has a different eye color; other
species of *Uroplatus* are significantly smaller
and are more easily distinguished from this
species

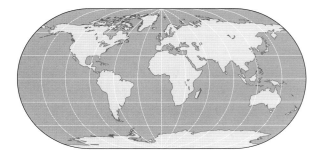

Giant Leaf-Tailed Gecko

Uroplatus fimbriatus

Madagascar is home to many unique and unusual animals, but none is more bizarre to look at than the giant leaf-tailed gecko, which has been described as an "animated gargoyle."

LIKE THE NORTHERN LEAF-TAILED GECKO from Australia, *Saltuarius cornutus*, the giant leaf-tailed gecko from Madagascar relies heavily on crypsis, or camouflage, to escape the notice of predators. Its colors and markings imitate the mottled rough bark of forest trees. It spends its days clinging to the trunk of a tree with its head pointing downward and its hind legs stretched out at an angle of about 45 degrees. Although it often rests in an exposed position, it can be almost impossible to see. It stays completely still even when approached at close quarters.

As well as blending in with the background, the gecko avoids detection by pressing itself close to the surface. Its flattened tail and the frilly fringes of skin along its jaws and flanks prevent shadows from forming. If it thinks it has been discovered, however, it pushes itself away from the trunk and opens its mouth wide, revealing its bright red tongue. Such intimidating displays and the gecko's strange appearance cause local people to fear it, believing it to be a devil named *taha-fisaka*.

Night Forays

The geckos come to life after dark and move away from their daytime retreats in search of food. In common with some other leaf-tailed geckos, their markings develop more contrast at night. Their movements are slow and deliberate; but if startled, they can move quite quickly.

Because of their size they can tackle most invertebrates and probably small vertebrates as well. Their method of catching prey is to pause with their limbs gathered beneath their body, leaning forward slightly at the same time. They study their prey from this position before lunging forward with great force and grabbing it in their jaws. This species has more teeth than any other lizard on earth.

After a night's activity a gecko will often return to the exact place where it rested the day before—there are even reports that by resting in the same place, the geckos can create bare patches on tree trunks that are otherwise covered in lichens.

Individuals are rarely found close together in nature, and these geckos are thought to be territorial. They wave their tail when they meet another member of their species and may vocalize, but such interactions have only been casually observed and are not fully understood. During courtship the male vibrates his tail rapidly before mating. Females lay a pair of spherical, hard-shelled eggs about four to five weeks after mating and bury them in leaf litter on the forest floor. At a constant 80°F (26°C) the eggs hatch after 77 to 84 days.

⬅ *A disturbed giant leaf-tailed gecko is an intimidating sight with its wide gape and brightly colored mouth. These geckos are among the largest in the world.*

The Relatives

There are 11 species in the genus *Uroplatus* from Madagascar and probably more yet to be discovered. Some are newly described—*U. pietschmanni* as recently as 2004. Several species are almost as large as the giant leaf-tailed gecko, but there are a number of smaller species. *Uroplatus phantasticus*, for example, grows to about 4 inches (10 cm) long. Its tail is shaped like a shriveling dead leaf, and it has a prominent ridge along its back and small spines over its eyes. The lined leaf-tailed gecko, *U. lineatus*, is more slender than other species and is tan to yellow in color with numerous fine lines running along its body. It is thought to live in bamboo forests—its color and markings provide effective camouflage. The mossy flat-tailed gecko, *U. sikorae*, is possibly the most effectively camouflaged of all species, however. This medium-sized species is marked with patches of scales in various colors mimicking the patches of green, white, and gray lichens and mosses that grow all over trees and branches in the rain forests. Even from a few inches away it can be almost impossible to make out this gecko's outline.

Common name Tokay gecko

Scientific name *Gekko gecko*

Subfamily Gekkoninae

Family Gekkonidae

Suborder Sauria

Order Squamata

Size From 8 in (20 cm) to 14 in (36 cm) long

Key features A large, heavy-bodied gecko with a massive head, prominent yellow or orange eyes, and a huge gape; conspicuous toe pads present; skin covered in small granular scales interspersed with raised tubercles; color bluish gray with evenly scattered spots of lighter blue and rust

Habits Naturally arboreal but also found on the walls of buildings; nocturnal

Breeding Female lays 2 (sometimes 3) spherical, hard-shelled eggs; eggs usually hatch after about 100 days

Diet Invertebrates of all sizes and small vertebrates, including other geckos

Habitat Forests, plantations, and buildings

Distribution Southeast Asia

Status Very common

Similar species The green-eyed gecko, *Gekko smithii,* is about the same size but gray in color with emerald-green eyes

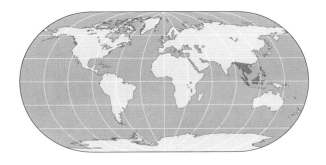

Tokay Gecko

Gekko gecko

The brightly colored tokay is the species that gives the whole family its common and scientific names. These large geckos make a raucous call that sounds, according to some listeners, like "gek-ko."

THE TOKAY GECKO IS ONE OF THE MOST VOCAL geckos. Its call can be heard for 100 yards (91 m) or more. While some people think the call sounds like "gek-ko," others interpret it as "toe-kay," hence its common name. Two tokays living near each other will have a "conversation" with calls echoing back and forth, not unlike the vocalizations of some frogs and toads.

This type of communication probably helps keep individual geckos spaced out and thereby ensures that they avoid competition. Calling is intensified during the main breeding season, when these geckos often call throughout the night. However, at other times of the year calling is less frequent, and they may be silent altogether at certain times. Their routine seems to vary from place to place, however, and some observers have noted that tokays call any time they are active.

Living With Humans

Tokays are forest species, living on vertical surfaces such as tree trunks and spending their days in cracks and behind loose bark. They have adapted very well to human activities, however, and are common around villages. Most homes will have a resident tokay, often living between the two layers of wooden boards around the outside of the house or behind pieces of furniture such as cupboards and closets. They are creatures of habit, and individuals will have favorite places to which they return regularly. They can even be relied on to emerge at roughly the same time every night.

⊕ *The jaws of the tokay gecko are strong, and its teeth are sharp, enabling it to eat quite large items of prey, such as this locust.*

As soon as the sun begins to fade, the tokays will creep out from their daytime hiding places. They move cautiously at first before coming right out and heading for a favorite hunting position. If they are unsuccessful, they will move on after a while to try their luck somewhere else, but they have a well-defined "beat" that they patrol and that they defend against other tokays.

If they are in an area where there are electric lights, they often wait nearby, taking advantage of the moths, cockroaches, and other insects that are attracted to them. If necessary, they will alter their routine slightly to move to a window with a light in it. Tokays will also prey on the smaller geckos that live around buildings, although populations seem to vary in this respect, and in some places they live peacefully side by side.

Geckos on the House

Geckos have adapted perhaps better than most reptiles to human development. The species with expanded toe pads that live naturally on tree trunks or rock faces have moved easily into buildings. They are a regular feature in most accommodation—even modern hotels and restaurants—in Asia and elsewhere. There are plenty of hiding places in the eaves of roofs or in thatch, and the invention of electric lights has been of great benefit to geckos because of the flying insects that are attracted to them. House geckos have been quick to exploit this, and it is not unusual to see half a dozen or more lying in wait on or near the lights as soon as they come on in the evening. Others chase back and forth across the ceiling, chattering to each other and occasionally squabbling over a moth or a cockroach.

For this reason the common name of "house gecko" has been applied to a large number of species, including several *Gekko* species. However, the experts at house occupancy are the half-fingered geckos, *Hemidactylus* species, such as Brook's house gecko, *H. brookii,* the common house gecko, *H. frenatus,* and Moreau's house gecko, *H. mabouia.* These species have also been introduced around the world, traveling as stowaways among lumber, building materials, and food produce. In particular, the common house gecko is found throughout practically the whole of the tropical and subtropical world, including Florida, Hawaii, Mexico, and most other Central American countries as well as the whole of the Pacific region. It is probably the most widespread and numerous reptile in the world.

Attack and Defense

Tokays usually wait on a wall near a light with their head pointing down, ready to snap up any suitable prey that lands nearby. If they are really hungry, they will stalk their prey for a short distance before rushing at it from about 12 inches (30 cm) away.

They have a large gape, powerful jaw muscles, and sharp teeth, all of which are adapted for crushing their prey but are equally suitable for defending themselves. Receiving a bite from a large tokay is an experience best avoided because they can easily draw blood and cause painful lacerations. Once their jaws

⊕ *The distinctive palm, or white-striped, gecko,* Gekko vittatus *from the Solomon Islands, has a single white stripe running along the center of its back.*

Tokay Relatives

There are 30 geckos belonging to the genus *Gekko*. Most of them are smaller than the tokay, but a few approach it in size. The palm, or white-striped, gecko, *G. vittatus*, occurs from India through to the Philippines and the Solomon Islands. It is strikingly marked with a bold cream or white line running up the center of its back and then dividing into two lines that reach almost to the angle of each jaw. This species is more slender and less aggressive than the tokay. The green-eyed gecko, *G. smithii*, is found throughout Southeast Asia, including on many islands. It can grow slightly larger than the tokay and is mottled grayish brown in color with large emerald-green eyes. It also has a very loud call and is known locally as the "tok-tok" lizard. Other members of the genus are smaller, are not as widespread, and do not vocalize as loudly. They range from India throughout Southeast Asia, China, Japan, and several Pacific Island groups. A number of new species have been described from Vietnam since the country opened up to scientific exploration in the 1980s.

are fastened around something, they are very difficult to dislodge.

Adult tokays have few enemies, but they are sometimes eaten by snakes, especially climbing species such as the flying snakes, *Chrysopelea*, and a variety of ratsnakes. They put up a good fight and often escape, sometimes losing their tail in the process. One observer saw a fight that lasted for three hours, with the gecko and the snake both gripping the other in its jaws. The fight only ended when the pair was disturbed.

Humans are the tokays' biggest threat, especially in places such as China, where they are dried and sold in markets for food. They are also thought to have medicinal properties or to act as aphrodisiacs. As a result, tokay numbers are declining in some large cities.

Family Groups

Tokays appear to live in small groups with a single adult male and a number of females living within a territory.

→ The green-eyed gecko, Gekko smithii, is similar to the tokay gecko. It comes from Southeast Asia, where its loud call has earned it the name of "tok-tok" lizard.

The male mates with any of these females. Depending on the climate where they live, breeding probably takes place throughout most of the year.

Females lay two (or occasionally three) spherical, hard-shelled eggs. They attach them to a vertical surface, often between two layers of material; it can be under loose bark in the wild, in cracks between boards, or even behind furniture and pictures in a building. Each female may lay several clutches during the course of a breeding season with an interval of about one month between each clutch. Since they often return to the same place to lay their eggs and several females may use the same site, entire eggs and the remains of hatched ones are often found together.

The hatching time for the eggs is highly variable—from 60 to 200 days. Some of the variation is undoubtedly due to temperature differences, and the majority of eggs hatch in about 100 days. This species has temperature-dependent sex determination (TDSD), in which eggs incubated at higher temperatures—around 85°F (30°C) or more—hatch into males.

The hatchlings of both sexes are more boldly marked than the adults. They are dark gray with large white spots arranged in rows across their body and they have black-and-white banded tails. The head is proportionately larger than that of the adults.

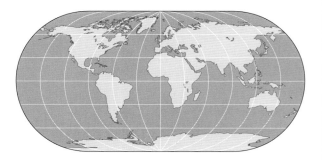

Common name Ashy gecko

Scientific name *Sphaerodactylus elegans*

Subfamily Sphaerodactylinae

Family Gekkonidae

Suborder Sauria

Order Squamata

Size 2.8 in (7.1 cm) long

Key features Head pointed and flattened; body and tail cylindrical with a speckled pattern of yellowish-brown markings on a darker background; markings sometimes run together to form stripes or parts of stripes, especially on the head; toe pads present on digits, but they are small and easily overlooked; juveniles are gray with dark crossbands and a reddish tail

Habits Diurnal and terrestrial or arboreal

Breeding Female lays a single hard-shelled egg; further detail unkown

Diet Small insects and spiders

Habitat Rarely seen away from buildings but thought to live naturally in forests and plantations

Distribution Cuba, Hispaniola; introduced to Florida

Status Common

Similar species All *Sphaerodactylus* species look similar; in Florida it is the only small gecko with many small pale spots covering the entire head, body, and tail; separation from other West Indian species can be very difficult

Ashy Gecko *Sphaerodactylus elegans*

The ashy gecko is a tiny lizard that often goes unnoticed. Nonetheless, it is a successful and adaptable colonizer and often occurs in houses and gardens.

THE ASHY GECKO IS NATIVE TO CUBA and Hispaniola but was introduced to Key West many years ago, probably on a shipment of wood or fruit. Since then it has spread up the Florida Keys and has also been seen on the Gulf Coast. In time it may spread from the south to many more parts of the state. Interestingly, there may be as many as 14 gecko species in Florida, but only one is native. This is another *Sphaerodactylus* species, the Florida reef gecko, *S. notatus*, found also in the south of the state and on the Dry Tortugas islands. It is thought to be native to the region, although related forms occur on Cuba and the Bahamas.

The ashy gecko tends to live around houses, especially on vertical walls. It is diurnal by nature but occasionally comes out at night to feed on insects that are attracted to an outside light. The reef gecko is more likely to occur on the ground among debris such as boards, coconut husks, and garbage. It is even smaller than the ashy gecko, and at 2.5 inches (6.3 cm) when fully grown, it is the smallest North American lizard.

Fast and Agile

The ashy gecko has minute granular scales. Those on the top of the tail are slightly rough, although the reason for this is not clear. *Sphaerodactylus* means "ball toes," and this gecko has very small pads with rounded surfaces. Since it is small and light, it does not need the adhesive power of some of the larger geckos. It is quick and agile, however, and difficult to catch.

In its native Cuba the ashy gecko often lives in houses, hiding behind furniture and pictures. It does not appear to have a voice,

⤒ *In Florida an ashy gecko sheds its skin. Unlike snakes, lizards usually shed their skin in pieces.*

⤏ *The genus* Gonatodes *contains 17 species of dwarf geckos distributed throughout the Central and northern South American region. This is a* Gonatodes ceciliae *male from Trinidad.*

their eggs in the same place, and the remains of many eggs are sometimes found together in especially favored places. Hatchlings are correspondingly small, barely 1 inch (2.5 cm) in length. They are light gray in color with several narrow, dark crossbands on their head, neck, and body. The bands extend onto the tail but become shorter and more like spots. The rest of the tail is rosy red in color. The difference between juveniles and adults is so great that they were once thought to belong to separate species.

and individuals recognize each other by tongue-licking.

Details of courtship are completely lacking, but females lay a single, pea-sized egg that has a hard shell. The egg can go through the female's cloaca because it is flexible when laid and only becomes hardened when exposed to air. Eggs are laid in cracks in wood or in small spaces among debris. Several females may lay

Dwarf Geckos

The ashy gecko is one of about 95 species in the genus *Sphaerodactylus*. Its stronghold is the Caribbean region, with most species occurring on the large and small islands and just a few reaching the mainland. Together with four other genera—*Coleodactylus* (five species), *Lepidoblepharis* (17 species), *Gonatodes* (17 species), and *Pseudogonatodes* (seven species)—they make up a group of dwarf geckos that are sometimes placed in a separate subfamily, the Sphaerodactylinae. All the members of this group occur in South or Central America, all are small, and all lay a single egg.

They are mostly diurnal, and some are brightly colored, especially the males. In the striped day gecko, *Gonatodes vittatus*, for example, males are tan in color with a wide, black-edged white stripe down the back and over the head between the eyes. Females have only faint traces of the stripe and are mottled brown. The yellow-headed gecko, *G. albogularis,* comes from Central America and many West Indian islands but, like the ashy gecko, has also made a home for itself in Florida. The males have a dark blue body and a tan or yellowish head, while the females have mottled brown bodies with a light collar. Colonies of these geckos live on the trunks of large forest trees.

Common name Moorish gecko
(common wall gecko, crocodile gecko)

Scientific name *Tarentola mauretanica*

Subfamily Gekkoninae

Family Gekkonidae

Suborder Sauria

Order Squamata

Size 6 in (15 cm) long

Key features Heavily built; head wide; mouth large;
large, slightly spiky scales on its back, sides,
and tail give it a roughened appearance; color
light or dark gray with darker bands across
the body and tail, most obvious in juveniles;
small red marks often present between its
toes caused by parasitic gecko mites

Habits Nocturnal, living on walls and rock faces; it
will also live among rocks on the ground;
occasionally basks during the day

Breeding Female lays up to 15 clutches of 1 or (more
commonly) 2 hard-shelled eggs; eggs hatch
after 44–75 days

Diet Invertebrates

Habitat Dry places, including stone and plaster walls,
tiles, cliffs, and woodpiles

Distribution Mediterranean (Spain, Portugal, coastal
regions of France, Italy, Greece, and North
Africa; also many large and small islands)

Status Very common

Similar species Other *Tarentola* species, from which it is
best distinguished by distribution; the other
Mediterranean gecko is the Turkish gecko,
Hemidactylus turcicus, which is smaller and
has a pale-pinkish, translucent skin

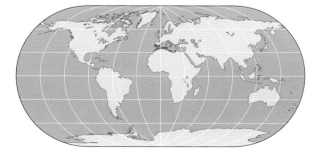

Moorish Gecko
Tarentola mauretanica

The nocturnal, climbing moorish gecko is sometimes known as the crocodile gecko because of its rough, spiky scales. For its size it is strong and heavily built.

ALTHOUGH THE MOORISH GECKO DOES MOST of its hunting at night, it occasionally basks during the day to raise its temperature and aid digestion. It typically sticks its head out from behind an object or from a crevice and basks with just part of its body exposed. The slightest movement toward it will send it scurrying back to cover. It has many enemies, including whip snakes (*Coluber* species), smooth snakes (*Coronella girondica*), egrets and ibises, weasels (*Mustela nivalis*), and small cats, including domestic cats. The latter probably kill more of these geckos than any other predator.

As night falls, the geckos venture out and may make their way to places where lights have attracted flying insects. They are aggressive feeders, and their diet includes scorpions, sow bugs, moths, beetles, and smaller lizards. Prey is taken with a rush and seized in their powerful jaws before being crushed and swallowed.

The Moorish gecko is an agile climber, moving easily across vertical glass surfaces and running across ceilings. Males do not tolerate each other and chase interlopers away, but several females and juveniles may live within a male's territory.

They use a wide range of calls to communicate with each other. The calls can be defensive, aggressive, or can indicate courtship behavior. Calling is often more frequent during the early part of the night as the geckos begin to move around.

⊕ *Moorish geckos will actively hunt down and eat any small invertebrate. This individual in Spain is preying on a moth.*

SEE ALSO Geckos 45:8; Snake, Western Whip 49:28

Successive Clutches

Breeding takes places throughout the warmer months of the year, and in North Africa it can be almost continuous, with just a short break in the winter. Females lay up to 15 clutches of eggs in a single year at intervals of about two weeks. Young females often lay single eggs before beginning to produce them in pairs as they themselves grow larger.

They bury the eggs in moist sand or soil at the base of stone walls or similar structures, using alternate hind feet to make a hole. The size of the hole depends on whether the female has one or two eggs to lay, and the entire process takes 10 minutes or more. As each egg is laid, the female catches it with her hind feet to break its fall before laying the second egg (if there is one) about a minute later. She fills in the hole by scraping with the front feet and smoothing over the surface. The eggs hatch after 44 to 75 days depending on temperature.

Tarantula Connections

The genus *Tarentola* gets its name from the Italian port of Taranto where it occurs. The same town gave its name to the *tarantella* dance and thence to the tarantula spider. Apart from the Moorish gecko, there are 18 species in the genus. The largest, *Tarentola albertschwartzi* from Jamaica, is probably extinct, since it is known from a single specimen collected in 1884 but not described until 1998 (it sat unnoticed for over 100 years in the National Museum of Scotland). Another large species, *T. gigas*, lives on the Cape Verde Islands, and several other species live on islands and archipelagos off the West African coast, including Madeira and the Canary Islands. One species, the American wall gecko, *T. americana*, occurs on Cuba and the Bahamas, its ancestors having presumably floated there on rafts many thousands of years ago.

Naming the genus after a port turned out to be very apt: The many wall gecko species on remote island groups owe their existence to individuals or groups that have made long and heroic sea voyages, perhaps clinging to pieces of driftwood or vegetation uprooted during a storm.

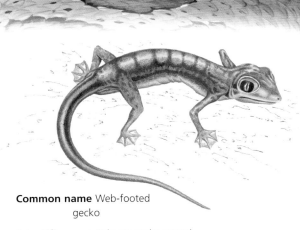

Common name Web-footed gecko

Scientific name *Palmatogecko rangei*

Subfamily Gekkoninae

Family Gekkonidae

Suborder Sauria

Order Squamata

Size From 4 in (10 cm) to 5 in (13 cm) long

Key features A delicate gecko with small scales and translucent, smooth skin; characterized by webbing between the toes and prominent, large, colorful eyes situated on top of the head; color pinkish above with faint netting of a darker shade and white below; the 2 colors meet abruptly along the flanks; limbs thin and spindly

Habits Terrestrial and nocturnal; escapes the daytime heat by resting in a burrow

Breeding Female lays several clutches each containing 2 hard-shelled eggs; eggs hatch after 55–90 days

Diet Small invertebrates, especially termites, crickets, grasshoppers, and beetles

Habitat Sand dunes

Distribution Namib Desert from the Richtersveld of South Africa to extreme southern Angola

Status Common in suitable habitat

Similar species The Kaoko web-footed gecko, *Palmatogecko vanzyli*, also lives in the Namib Desert but is restricted to gravel plains in the north; it is similar to the web-footed gecko, but only its hind feet are webbed

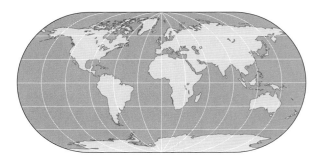

LIZARDS

Web-Footed Gecko
Palmatogecko rangei

Despite its frail appearance, the little web-footed gecko makes its home in the Namib Desert, one of the world's harshest and most inhospitable environments.

THE WEB-FOOTED GECKO RARELY, if ever, drinks from standing water because rain is almost unheard of in the places where it lives. Instead, it drinks the droplets of water that condense on its skin during fogs that occur on about 100 nights of the year. It also gets moisture from the insects it eats. It catches them at night by stalking them across the sand dunes where it lives.

Because the dunes are moving due to the constant wind, the gecko is unable to set up a permanent home. It digs a new burrow in the sand every day, about 20 inches (50 cm) deep, where its spends the daytime sheltering from the heat. It emerges long after sundown when the temperature has fallen and forages over the sand. It is regularly active at temperatures as low as 55°F (13°C)—one individual was found when the temperature had dropped almost to freezing point.

On the surface of the dunes the gecko's webbed feet keep it from sinking into the fine sand, acting like snowshoes to take its weight. Although the surface of the sand cools rapidly once the sun has disappeared, the sand temperature just below the surface remains steady at about 75 to 85°F (24–30°C).

Night Vision

Web-footed geckos forage for nocturnal invertebrates and eat large numbers of termites as well as crickets, grasshoppers, and beetles. Their huge eyes allow them to hunt in almost total darkness. Their most important predators are also nocturnal and include golden moles, *Eremitalpa granti*, owls, small vipers (especially

⊕ *At daybreak a pair of web-footed geckos raise themselves on their front legs and use their enormous eyes to overcome poor visibility in the Namib Desert.*

the Namib sidewinder, *Bitis peringueyi*), and the giant ground gecko, *Chondrodactylus angulifer*. Web-footed geckos are almost defenseless but will raise themselves up on stiffened legs, arch their back, and thrash their tail from side to side if threatened. In the case of extreme provocation they may shed their tail, but they do this reluctantly, perhaps because the food stored in it is more precious than normal in such a barren environment.

Breeding

Male web-footed geckos can be identified instantly by a pair of bulges (the hemipenal bulges) at the base of the tail. Males vocalize with a series of about five low-pitched chirps; this is thought to be a territorial call. Courtship has not been observed, but females lay two very brittle, thin-shelled eggs during the summer from November to March, burying them in a short tunnel that they dig in the

Wonders of the Desert

The Namib Desert is thought to be the oldest desert in the world; as a result, there has been plenty of time for interesting and unique plants and animals to evolve. The *Palmatogecko* species are excellent examples. The Kaoko web-footed gecko, *P. vanzyli*, is the only other member of the genus. It has webbing on its hind feet, but its front feet have normal, clawed toes. It is not as well known as its more common relative, *P. rangei*, because it lives only in Kaokoland in the far northwest of Namibia, a remote and rarely visited region. It prefers gravel plains rather than sand dunes. But, like *P. rangei*, it retreats into tunnels during the day. It uses its front feet to dig the tunnels and its webbed hind feet to shovel the sand to one side.

sand. They lay a number of clutches—two captive females produced a total of 30 eggs between them in a single season. The eggs hatch after about 55 to 90 days depending on temperature, and the hatchlings measure about 1.5 inches (3.8 cm) in length.

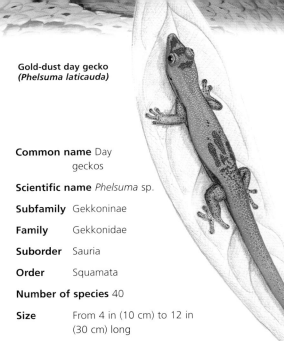

Gold-dust day gecko
(*Phelsuma laticauda*)

Common name Day geckos

Scientific name *Phelsuma* sp.

Subfamily Gekkoninae

Family Gekkonidae

Suborder Sauria

Order Squamata

Number of species 40

Size From 4 in (10 cm) to 12 in (30 cm) long

Key features Expanded toe pads present; eyes smaller than in other geckos; pupils circular; scales on the back small and granular; color mostly bright green often with red markings; a few of the larger species are dull olive or grayish green; both sexes usually the same color

Habits Arboreal and diurnal

Breeding Females lay 2 hard-shelled eggs and either stick them to a vertical surface, hide them in a hollow stem, or bury them in the ground; eggs hatch after 35–60 days

Diet Insects, fruit, and nectar

Habitat Forests, plantations, and clearings, often on the trunks of palms and other large trees; some species found around human habitats, others restricted to undisturbed forests

Distribution Southwest Africa (1 species), East Africa, Madagascar, the Comoros Islands, Mascarene Islands, and other Indian Ocean island groups as far east as the Andaman Islands

Status Mostly fairly common, but some species live in very restricted habitats

Similar species Effectively none; a few other brightly colored geckos either do not occur in the same region or are not bright green

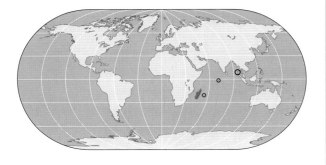

Day Geckos

Phelsuma sp.

Of the 900 or so species of geckos the majority are dull-colored, nocturnal lizards, but the day geckos from the Indian Ocean region contradict that description on both counts.

FORTY SPECIES and many more subspecies belonging to the genus *Phelsuma* range from the African mainland to the Andaman Islands. *Phelsuma* species are generally referred to as day geckos. Most are brightly colored, usually in greens and reds. They are active during the day and adapt well to a variety of conditions.

Members of the genus characteristically have large eyes with round pupils, resulting from their diurnal activity pattern. They also exhibit visual displays as opposed to relying on the vocalizations used by many nocturnal geckos. Males are larger than females in every species studied so far, probably because natural selection has favored larger males that can defend territories more effectively. In only one species, however, is there any noticeable difference in the colors of the sexes. This is *P. modesta* from southern Madagascar.

Filling a Niche

Their adaptability is probably the key to the day geckos' success. As a group they have moved into an ecological niche—being small, agile, brightly colored, and diurnal—usually occupied by other lizards. They take the place of, for example, the anole lizards in South and Central America and the wall lizards in Europe and the Mediterranean region.

One can only assume that the lack of competition from lizards of this type allowed them to switch to a diurnal lifestyle sometime after their arrival on Madagascar, after which it was only a matter of time before they evolved

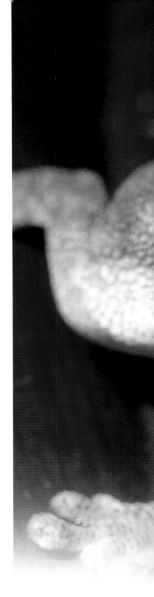

↑ *Abbott's day gecko,* Phelsuma abbotti, *can be found among low trees and bushes on Aldabra Atoll in the Seychelles and on the island of Nosy Bé off northwest Madagascar. This small lizard reaches a maximum total length of 5.5 inches (1.4 cm).*

 SEE ALSO Anole, Green **44**:106; Geckos **45**:8; Wall Lizards **45**:58

eventually across the Indian Ocean to other islands.

The Pemba day gecko, *P. parkeri* from Pemba Island off the coast of Tanzania in East Africa, is intermediate in appearance between the dull mainland species, *P. occellata*, and the bright Madagascan and other Indian Ocean species. However, the dull green day gecko, *P. dubia*, which is also found along the Tanzanian coast and on Zanzibar, was probably introduced there, since its main distribution lies along the west coast of Madagascar and on the Comoros Islands situated between Madagascar and the mainland. Both these day geckos are quite dull in color. The Comoros Islands are home to five other species of day geckos. One of them, the gold-dust, or flat-tailed, day gecko, *P. laticauda*, also occurs on Madagascar, while the other four are endemic to the Comoros Islands.

⊕ *One of the largest day geckos,* Phelsuma madagascariensis grandis *from western Madagascar, measures up to 12 inches (30 cm) long.*

into different species with myriad forms. Their main center of distribution is still Madagascar, where over 20 species are known, 16 of them endemic to the island. Their overall distribution is much wider than this, however.

The Namaqua day gecko, *P. ocellata*, is an oddball species. It lives on the west coast of South Africa in a dry, semidesert environment where it runs around on rock outcrops and shelters under large flakes of exfoliating rock. In contrast to most other members of the genus, it is not green but light grayish brown with scattered lighter and darker spots. Some herpetologists think that this species does not belong in the genus, while others believe it is the survivor from a group of geckos that were once more widespread in southern Africa and that spread eastward to Madagascar and

The eastern extreme of the geographical range for the day geckos is the Andaman Island group off the west coast of Thailand. *Phelsuma andamanensis* may have drifted to these remote islands on detritus or vegetation (a process known as rafting), but this seems unlikely. Or it may have been present when the islands broke away from the main Gondwanaland landmass and drifted east. Its closest relatives are probably the two day gecko species living on the Seychelles, the Seychelles day gecko, *P. astriata,* and the Seychelles giant day gecko, *S. sundbergi.* Once part of Gondwanaland,

33

the Seychelles are granite islands that took a selection of reptiles and amphibians with them when they split away and drifted eastward, including the Seychelles frogs, *Sooglossus* and *Nesomantis* species, and seven species of caecilians.

Species in Crisis

The Mascarene Islands east of Madagascar, consisting of Mauritius, Réunion, Rodriguez, and a number of smaller islands (notably Round Island), also have a selection of day geckos. Two species, the ornate day gecko, *P. ornata,* and the blue-tailed day gecko, *P. cepediana*, are notable for their brilliant coloration.

Round Island is notorious for its habitat destruction, with the loss (or near loss) of many species. One of the two boas living there has become extinct in recent times and the other is Critically Endangered (IUCN). The Round Island day gecko is *P. guentheri*, a large, dull species that has been saved from the brink of extinction thanks to a last-minute effort to reverse habitat destruction on the island (by shooting all the goats and rabbits) and setting up breeding programs in zoos.

Unfortunately, time has already run out for the two day geckos from Rodriguez—*P. gigas* and Newton's day gecko, *P. edwardnewtoni,* are presumed extinct mainly because of habitat destruction, but helped along by predation from introduced rats. *Phelsuma gigas* was the largest species, with a head and body measuring 7.5 inches (19 cm) and a total length of 15 inches (38 cm) or more. It is only known from fossil remains, but Newton's day gecko was last seen in 1917, and six preserved museum specimens survive.

Day Geckos in Madagascar

The Madagascan species, which make up the bulk of the genus, show variation in color, size, and habits. Madagascar can be divided roughly into a humid sector (mainly along the east coast and the north) and a drier region (in the south and west). The distribution of the various species correlates well with this. In other words,

each species lives in either a humid or a dry region. However, there are exceptions that occur within both environments.

Humid regions are often covered with rain forests, and species living there tend to be bright green in color and often have bright-red spots and markings on their backs. Those from drier places, however, tend to be grayish green. This difference reflects their camouflage requirements; but having said that, some of the brightest species easily eclipse the coloration of the foliage among which they live. It seems that selective pressures that have pushed them toward bright colors for the purposes of species recognition and communication have tempered the need for camouflage in some species.

Many day geckos live on tree trunks rather than among foliage. The largest Madagascan species, *P. madagascariensis*, for example, is almost unbelievably colorful. It has brilliant-green upper surfaces marked with bright-red spots and netting on its back. The exact shape of the markings varies according to subspecies. However, the subspecies that live in the humid west of the island, *P. m. madagascariensis* and *P. m grandis*, are brighter than the one from the slightly drier southeast, *P. m. kochi*, the latter being one of the few species that occurs almost islandwide.

The well-named peacock day gecko, *P. quadriocellata*, is bright green and has the added attraction of a black eyespot ringed in bright blue just behind its front legs. Other bright species include the lined day gecko, *P. lineata*, which has a dark line running down each flank, and the gold-dust day gecko,

⊕ *Listed as Vulnerable by the IUCN, this juvenile Standing's day gecko,* Phelsuma standingi *from Madagascar, is restricted to a small region in the southwestern part of the island.*

⊖ *The strikingly marked gold-dust day gecko,* Phelsuma laticauda, *is found in large numbers in humid areas of northern Madagascar.*

P. laticauda, which has a dense cluster of small, gold-colored scales on the nape of its neck.

Species from the west and south include the modest day gecko, *P. modesta*, in which the males are fairly bright bluish green with red markings, but the females are dull grayish blue. There is also the large Standing's day gecko, *P. standingi*, which is bluish gray with dark netting on its head. Hatchlings of this species are pale blue with reddish-brown crossbands, but the reason for this is not known. Similarly, the thick-tailed day gecko, *P. mutabilis,* and *P. breviceps*, which has no common name, are both gray or brown. Both are restricted to the south of the island. *Phelsuma breviceps* is also of interest because its skin is very fragile and comes off if it is grasped by a predator, helping the lizard escape. The same trick is used by other geckos from the same part of the world, notably the bronze geckos, *Ailuronyx* from the Seychelles, the fish-scale geckos, *Geckolepis* from Madagascar, and the thin-skinned gecko, *Pachydactylus kladoderma* from South Africa.

Climbing and Feeding

Like many other geckos, the day geckos have adhesive pads on their toes and are highly efficient climbers. In dry regions and on small oceanic islands they live mostly on the trunks of palm trees, and in more humid places they also live on the trunks of forest trees.

Day geckos eat a wide variety of small invertebrates, including flies, grasshoppers, and spiders, but they also have a sweet tooth. They will lick the juices from overripe fruit, and they also visit flowers to lap up the nectar. In doing so, they may act as pollinators. In captivity they like honey and sugarcubes, which they will visit regularly until there is none left.

Some species are adapted to man-made habitats and can be found on the walls of buildings and on ornamental plants in gardens. Unlike many of Madagascar's reptiles, some day geckos, such as *P. madagascariensis* and

P. lineata, may have benefited from forest clearances, since they are more commonly seen around villages, farms, and plantations than in more natural habitats. However, they probably represent a minority (albeit a conspicuous one) of species, and the ranges of several species that prefer primary forests are dwindling due to habitat destruction—some are restricted to single localities. The yellow-headed day gecko, *P. klemmeri*, for example, is a stunningly beautiful small species that was only described in 1990 and lives exclusively in the coastal Sambirano region of northwestern Madagascar. Its back is bluish gray with a pair of wide turquoise lines running down each side, and its head is bright sulfur yellow. It lives in bamboo forests, where temperature and humidity are high throughout the year.

Territorial Encounters

In all the species that have been studied, interactions between individuals take the form of cautious head-to-head approaches, often accompanied by sideways tail waving. If they are two males, one will usually back off, but otherwise they may fight. Females are also territorial but less so, unless they are guarding eggs or a favored egg-laying site. Matings take place for extended periods, the length of which depends on the species and its distribution. For example, the southern African species breed in the spring, but tropical species probably breed at almost any time of the year.

Egg Gluers and Egg Hiders

Females lay two eggs (rarely just one). They can be divided into two groups as far as the egg-laying method is concerned. In one group of species the females glue their eggs to a suitable surface, usually a vertical area such as the underside of a piece of loose bark. Females in the other group do not lay sticky eggs. Instead, they catch their eggs with their back feet as they lay them and hold them until they become hard. These females deposit eggs in crevices such as the hollow tubes of bamboo stems. A

Other "Day" Geckos

Day geckos belonging to the genus *Phelsuma* are unique. There are other geckos that are active during the day, however, and they are sometimes called "day" geckos too, especially in the countries in which they live. About 17 species of dwarf geckos, *Lygodactylus*, occur in Madagascar alongside the *Phelsuma* species. They are mostly diurnal, although some species are also active in the evening. They have round pupils, but their bodies are not brightly colored—they have markings that make them hard to see when they are resting on branches or bark.

The genus *Lygodactylus* also occurs in Africa, where most of its representatives are also gray or brown in color, although the males of some are more brightly marked. Those of the white-headed dwarf gecko, *L. picturatus*, for instance, have a cream head and neck boldly marked with a dark brown pattern. They also have a bluish-gray tail and body. The yellow-headed dwarf gecko, *L. luteopicturatus*, is more colorful still: Its head, neck, and chest are bright yellow with dark markings, and the rest of its body, limbs, and tail are pale blue-gray. Both of these species come from Kenya and Tanzania. The show-stopper, however, is the turquoise dwarf gecko, *L. williamsi*, known only from the Kimbozi Forest, Tanzania. Males of this endangered species are bright blue with a faint pattern of darker lines on their head and flanks. The females are only slightly less colorful than the males.

The New Zealand geckos belonging to the genus *Naultinus* parallel the *Phelsuma* species in many ways, being diurnal, colorful, and about the same size, but they belong to a different family of geckos, the Diplodactylidae. They are quite slow moving and live in shrubs rather than on vertical surfaces. More significantly, they give birth to live young. Finally, the many small "day" geckos belonging to the genera *Sphaerodactylus* and *Gonatodes* from South and Central America are active during the day, have round pupils, and some of them are colorful.

⊕ *The common green gecko,* Naultinus elegans, *of which this individual is a yellow form, is endemic to New Zealand. It belongs to the Diplodactylidae but parallels the day geckos in being colorful and diurnal and feeding on fruit and flowers as well as insects.*

few species bury their eggs. As far as anyone knows, all the species living on the Mascarene Islands and some of the Madagascan species are "egg gluers" (they stick the eggs to a vertical surface), whereas all the others are nongluers—they hide them in a hollow stem or bury them in the ground

The eggs hatch in about 35 to 60 days, although this varies with temperature. As a rule, those of the larger species take longer than those of the smaller species. At least some species, and possibly all, have temperature-dependent sex determination (TDSD), in which temperatures of 81°F (27°C) or less produce female hatchlings and those of 86°F (30°C) or more produce males.

Protection

Day geckos are very popular in captivity. One species, Standing's day gecko, *P. standingi*, is listed as Vulnerable (IUCN). CITES has placed all the species on Appendix II except the Round Island day gecko, *P. guentheri*, which is on Appendix I. (Appendix II species are not thought to be under as much threat as those on Appendix I, but they may become so if trade is not regulated.) International trade in these species is monitored by a licensing system to ensure that trade can be sustained without harming wild populations. Unfortunately, the status of many species is not known, and large numbers of day geckos have been exported from Madagascar over a long period of time.

Common name Barking gecko

Scientific name *Ptenopus garrulus*

Subfamily Gekkoninae

Family Gekkonidae

Suborder Sauria

Order Squamata

Size 4 in (10 cm) long

Key features Chunky gecko with a rounded head, blunt snout, and large, bulging eyes; face appears to have a permanent "grin"; toes lack adhesive pads but have a fringe of pointed scales along the edges; back, head, and tail are brown, gray, or reddish brown with intricate marblings of light and dark spots; underside is white; male has a yellow throat

Habits Nocturnal and terrestrial

Breeding Female lays 2 hard-shelled eggs; further details unknown

Diet Small invertebrates such as termites, ants, and small beetles

Habitat Desert flats with hard-packed sand or gravely surfaces

Distribution Southern Africa (central and northwestern South Africa, most of Namibia and Central Botswana as far as extreme southern Zimbabwe)

Status Common in suitable habitat

Similar species 2 other barking geckos from the same region, Carp's barking gecko, *P. carpi*, and Koch's barking gecko, *P. kochi*, have restricted ranges in the Namib Desert

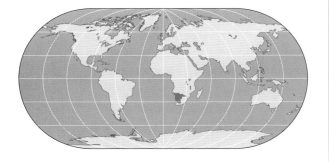

Barking Gecko

Ptenopus garrulus

Large parts of the Karoo, Kalahari, and Namib Deserts resound with the clicking calls of barking geckos as soon as the sun goes down. The name garrulus *suits them—they can be very talkative.*

THE LITTLE BARKING GECKOS ARE USUALLY HEARD but not seen. Males sit at the entrance of a burrow and call during the early part of each evening in spring and summer to attract a mate and to advertise their territory. The sound they make is best likened to two pebbles being tapped together repeatedly ("tock, tock, tock") and is not a "bark" at all. The number of "tocks" varies from one place to another and can be just one or as many as 13—five is typical.

Secret Passages

The slightest disturbance sends the geckos ducking back into their burrow, where they remain for several minutes before reemerging to continue calling. The burrows can be very complex, with blind passages and side branches running up toward the surface. If they are pursued into their burrow by a snake, for instance, they may escape onto the surface by breaking through one of the concealed exits. Other predators include owls and meerkats.

In regions that are largely covered by sand dunes, such as much of the Namib Desert, these geckos live in the hard-packed, pebbly plains between the dunes. They dig a permanent burrow between the embedded stones. In other places, including dry riverbeds, they burrow in pure sand or silt, but only if it is the right consistency, since they are unable to dig tunnels in loose, windblown sand. If the habitat is suitable, they live in extensive colonies, and in open landscapes their chorus echoes for several hundred yards. It is one of the more evocative sounds of southwestern Africa, signaling sunset.

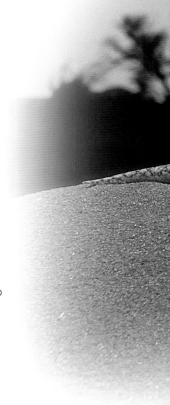

⬆ *Sunset is a busy time for barking geckos. They leave their burrows to find mates and look for food.*

Family and Neighbors

Two other barking geckos, Carp's barking gecko, *Ptenopus carpi*, and Koch's gecko, *P. kochi*, live along the narrow coastal fringes of the Namib Desert, making their burrows between dunes and in dry riverbeds. Their markings differ slightly from those of the more common species (*P. garrulus*), but their lifestyles are broadly similar.

In the same region there are two other notable geckos. The web-footed gecko, *Palmatogecko rangei*, lives a nomadic life on shifting sand dunes, digging a fresh burrow every morning, whereas the giant ground gecko, *Chondrodactylus angulifer*, is a larger species that seems to prefer slightly rockier microhabitats. Neither species has adhesive pads on the tips of their toes, since they do not climb. Throughout the whole region the dominant gecko genus is *Pachydactylus*, the thick-toed geckos. A number of species, such as the Marico gecko, *P. mariquensis,* and the rough-scaled gecko, *P. rugosus*, lead lives similar to the other ground-dwelling geckos, differing only in microhabitat preferences.

Fringed Fingers and Toes

Barking geckos have long claws that lack any form of adhesive pads. Instead, each digit has a fringe of long, pointed scales that help the gecko gain traction on loose sand or soil. They have a relatively slow and deliberate gait, stalking across the surface and pausing frequently to search for food. If they are disturbed in the open, they freeze, and their camouflage makes them very hard to see. In areas where roads run through the colonies, they are often seen on the surface, possibly because their prey is easier to see here or perhaps simply by chance. If they are picked up, they squeak and often attempt to bite.

Common name Kuhl's flying gecko
(Kuhl's parachute gecko)

Scientific name *Ptychozoon kuhli*

Subfamily Gekkoninae

Family Gekkonidae

Suborder Sauria

Order Squamata

Size 8 in (20 cm) long

Key features A frilly gecko; a flap of skin is present along the flanks between the front and hind limbs, and there is a scalloped frill on the edges of the tail; feet are webbed, and toes have adhesive pads; head, body, and tail are brown, gray, or olive in color with broken bands and patches of darker coloration, making the gecko well camouflaged

Habits Arboreal and nocturnal

Breeding Female lays 2 hard-shelled eggs; eggs hatch after about 100 days

Diet Insects and spiders

Habitat Rain forests with high humidity; also enters houses

Distribution Southeastern Asia (India—Nicobar Islands—Myanmar, southern Thailand, Malaysian Peninsula, Borneo, Sumatra, and Java)

Status Common

Similar species Apart from 5 other species of flying geckos, the species is very distinctive

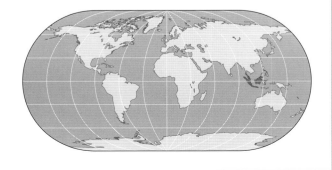

Kuhl's Flying Gecko

Ptychozoon kuhli

Southeast Asia is home to Kuhl's flying gecko and to a number of other "flying' reptiles," including snakes, frogs, and lizards.

FLYING, OR GLIDING, is not a widespread trait in reptiles. Only the flying geckos, *Ptychozoon*, the flying lizards, *Draco* species, and the flying snakes, *Chrysopelea*, have mastered it. All of them—39 species in total—come from the rain forests of Southeast Asia. One other lizard, the African blue-tailed tree lizard, *Holaspis guentheri* (sometimes regarded as two separate species), is thought to glide, but among the vast array of lizards in South and Central America, for instance, not one has taken to the air.

Some authorities think that the characteristics of the Asian rain forests, specifically the way in which the trees are spaced, may have contributed to the evolution of these "flying" forms. Tall, straight, hardwood trees (family Dipterocarpaceae) dominate many Asian forests, and the almost totally closed canopy shuts out light and prevents a shrubby understory from forming. By contrast, American and African rain-forest trees have more branches, and the forest takes on a more "crowded" character. In simple terms Asian rain forests are generally easy to walk through compared with South American ones.

Mastering "Flight"

No reptiles or amphibians are capable of powered flight. But by using flaps and flanges or by altering their body shape, some species can "glide" with a degree of control. The flying lizards, *Draco*, for example, always land head-up on the tree trunk they are aiming for by tucking their hind limbs under their body at the last minute so that they "stall." The flying snakes, *Chrysopelea*, can change direction by moving their bodies in a sinuous manner while they are gliding, and the flying geckos can even

⊕ *This closeup of the front part of Kuhl's flying gecko shows the head detail and the heavily webbed front feet. The dull brown color of its head and body provide good camouflage against the bark of a tree.*

change direction, using their tails as rudders, and head back in the direction they came from.

Gliding in Kuhl's gecko is accomplished by means of heavily webbed feet and a fringe that runs around the edge of its tail. It also has a flap of skin along each of its flanks. During extended flights air pressure causes them to spread out as well. Unlike the flying lizards, the gecko has no control over the erection or folding of these flaps.

The flaps and frills almost certainly arose to enhance the gecko's camouflage and not for the purpose of flight. The gecko is colored and marked to match the lichenous branches and trunks on which it rests, and the flaps act as a cloak to eliminate shadows. When a Kuhl's gecko lands after a glide, it immediately "freezes" so that any predators that may be watching its movements lose sight of it. Again, this is unlike the flying lizard, which immediately runs up the tree trunk to regain the height lost through the glide. Like most

geckos, Kuhl's flying gecko has adhesive pads at the tips of its toes that enable it to climb smooth surfaces, and also like many species, it sometimes occurs in houses and buildings.

Breeding

Male Kuhl's flying geckos are territorial and fight off intruders. Females apparently mate at any time of the year, although there may be

Who Was Kuhl?

Dr. Heinrich Kuhl was a German naturalist who lived from 1796 to 1821 and spent time in the East Indies. His short stay in the region was productive, since his name became associated with several fish, a frog, a lizard, a bird, and a mammal. As well as Kuhl's flying gecko, his name is celebrated in the kuhli loach, *Acanthophthalmus kuhli*, Kuhl's stingray, *Dasyatis kuhlii*, Kuhl's creek frog, *Limnonectes kuhlii*, Kuhl's lory, *Vini kuhlii*, and Kuhl's deer, *Axis kuhlii*. A family of Indo-Pacific marine fishes, the Kuhlidae, or flagtails, is also named after him. (The variation in the spelling of *kuhli* reflects the way it was spelled when each species was named.) *Ptychozoon* comes from two Greek words: *ptukhos*, meaning a fold, which refers to the fold of skin down the gecko's sides, and *-zoon*, meaning a living thing, or animal.

regional differences depending on climate. The eggs are usually laid in pairs, and a female can lay clutches every three or four weeks. They glue them to a suitable surface, often behind bark, and the eggs take about 100 days to hatch. The hatchlings are perfect replicas of the parents, complete with flaps and frills, and measure about 1.8 inches (4.5 cm) in total length. They grow quickly and can reach sexual maturity in less than one year.

Other *Ptychozoon* Species

There are six species in the genus altogether. One of them, *P. trinotaterra*, was only recently described and comes from Thailand and Vietnam, but the others have been known for at least 100 years. Four of them (*P. horsefieldii*, *P. intermedium*, *P. kuhli*, and *P. lionotum*) are quite widespread across the forests of Asia, and some overlap each other in places. *Ptychozoon rhacophorus*, however, is known only from Kina Balu, North Borneo, at an altitude of 2,100 feet (640 m). All these species look as though they could glide (and all are called parachute or flying geckos), but apart from *P. kuhli*, only *P. lionotum* has been seen to do so.

⊝ *As it takes to the air, the flaps and frills on the body and tail of Kuhl's flying gecko spread out to allow it to glide between resting places on forest trees.*

Taking to the Air

There are other types of gliding animals in Asian forests. Many frogs of the genus *Rhacophorus* use heavily webbed feet to "parachute" to lower levels. There are also flying squirrels, including 14 species in Borneo alone. Two species of flying "lemurs," *Cynocephalus variegatus* from Borneo and west Malaysia, and *C. volans* from the Philippines, are distinct from true lemurs (which live only on Madagascar) and are placed in an order of their own, the Dermoptera, meaning "skin-winged."

The Pteropodidae is the family to which flying foxes, or fruit bats, belong. About 166 species of these large, ungainly, fruit-eating bats are recognized. Apart from some species from Australia and a few others from Indian Ocean islands, they too are confined to South and Southeast Asia.

Common name Golden-tailed gecko

Scientific name *Diplodactylus taenicauda*

Family Diplodactylidae

Suborder Sauria

Order Squamata

Size 4.7 in (12 cm) long

Key features Head and body gray and black with a network of fine gray lines enclosing black spots of varying sizes; a bright orange stripe runs along the top of the tail; eyes also bright orange; toes end in small pads consisting of a pair of rounded scales with a small claw positioned between them

Habits Arboreal and nocturnal

Breeding Female lays 2 parchment-shelled eggs; in captivity eggs hatch after 52–77 days

Diet Small invertebrates

Habitat Dry forests and sparse eucalyptus woodlands

Distribution Australia (eastern Queensland)

Status Common in suitable habitat

Similar species There are other *Diplodactylus* species with similar size and body shapes, but none has the distinctive markings of this species

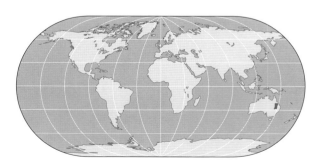

Golden-Tailed Gecko

Diplodactylus taenicauda

The golden-tailed gecko is a spectacularly beautiful small gecko with an unusual defense system—it secretes a sticky, smelly, foul-tasting fluid from pores in its tail to deter predators.

THE TAIL OF THE GOLDEN-TAILED GECKO has a number of chambers, each containing a small quantity of a sticky substance. When the gecko is threatened, it first tries to intimidate by opening its mouth wide and swinging its tail toward the aggressor. If that does not work, powerful muscles surrounding the chambers contract, causing the surrounding skin to rupture and the fluid to escape forcefully for up to 18 inches (46 cm). At the same time, the gecko swings its tail from side to side to make sure the substance is spread around well. The latexlike material quickly coagulates and becomes sticky, making it difficult to wipe off. After the attack the gecko cleans any remaining fluid from its tail by licking it repeatedly.

The golden-tailed gecko is not the only species to use this means of defense: 14 other members of its genus also have tail glands, and they are all sometimes placed in a separate genus, *Strophurus*, for this very reason. The remaining 24 species in the genus lack these glands. In the case of the golden-tailed gecko scientists believe that the brightly colored tail and the boldly marked body pattern act as warning signals.

Hatchling and juvenile golden-tailed geckos lack the bright-orange markings and are probably unable to squirt fluid. Their best means of defense is to remain camouflaged. Other species that bear tail glands, including the spiny-tailed gecko, *Diplodactylus ciliaris*, the western spiny-tailed gecko, *D. spinigerus*, and Williams's gecko, *D. williamsi*, have prominent spines on their tails, presumably to warn of their secret "weapon."

Strangely, all these "squirters" readily part with their tails (like most other geckos) if they are grabbed. However, the tail grows back very quickly. The fluid-producing chambers are thought to have evolved from similar chambers that in other geckos are used to store fat in readiness for hibernation or famine. The golden-tailed gecko and its close relatives have exchanged the fat-storing function for a defensive one.

Lifestyle and Breeding

The golden-tailed gecko lives in arid parts of Queensland, where daytime temperatures can exceed 95°F (35°C) in summer, and nighttime winter temperatures often fall below freezing. They may be active throughout the year, although very cold temperatures cause them to remain in hiding and to stop feeding for days or even weeks on end. They live and feed among pine, wattle, and

eucalyptus trees, sheltering by day under flaking bark and in hollow trunks and branches.

They can reach sexual maturity in under a year, so the young from one season's eggs can breed the next season, although most require two seasons to mature. They begin to breed in early spring, and females lay the first pair of eggs about 10 to 20 days after mating. They choose a humid place for this because the parchmentlike shells are permeable, and the eggs dry out quickly if the environment is too arid. The females may come down to the ground to find a suitable damp place.

Kept at a constant 82°F (28°C), the eggs take from 52 to 77 days to hatch in captivity, by which time the female will have laid one or two more clutches. Under ideal conditions (in other words, with plenty of food) females produce clutches every 20 days or so for four or five months. It is doubtful, however, that they are as prolific as this in the wild.

⊕ *The spiny-tailed gecko,* Diplodactylus ciliaris, *is similar to the golden-tailed gecko, but it has distinctive spines on its tail and above the eyes. Its body coloration is usually brown or gray and resembles bark.*

⊕ *Juvenile golden-tailed geckos are unable to squirt fluid from their tail and rely on camouflage colors of gray and black to avoid detection.*

Common name Northern leaf-tailed gecko

Scientific name *Saltuarius cornutus* (previously *Phyllurus cornutus*)

Family Diplodactylidae

Suborder Sauria

Order Squamata

Size Up to 13 in (33 cm) long

Key features Body slender and flattened; head triangular; limbs and digits spindly; tail shaped like a leaf or shield with a short spike at the end; feet have claws but no toe pads; each flank has a fold and a series of frilly or spiny scales; color brown, gray, or olive with a row of large pale blotches down the back; can be very hard to see when resting on a lichen-covered branch or tree trunk

Habits Arboreal and nocturnal

Breeding Female lays 2 parchment-shelled eggs; further details unknown

Diet Invertebrates

Habitat Rain forests and wet temperate forests

Distribution Australia (northeastern Queensland)

Status Common

Similar species *Saltuarius saleborus* from the same region is almost indistinguishable but has rough scales on its throat and a longer spiny extension to the tail; there are 11 other leaf-tailed geckos, including several only recently described, but they have less flattened tails

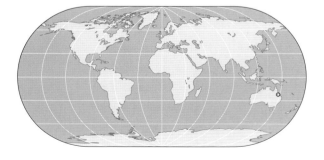

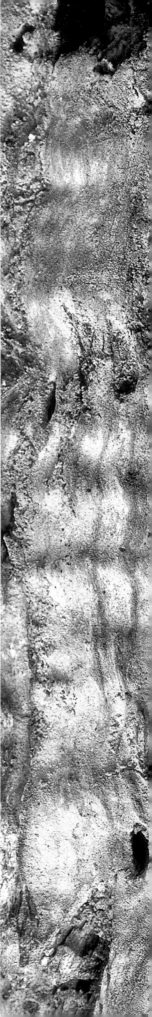

LIZARDS

Northern Leaf-Tailed Gecko

Saltuarius cornutus

The unusual shape of its tail, which provides excellent camouflage against a tree trunk, gives the northern leaf-tailed gecko its common name. Its mottled appearance also makes it hard to spot.

AUSTRALIA'S LEAF-TAILED GECKOS are highly specialized lizards whose biology is only just becoming known. Until 15 years ago only four species were identified, but there are now 13. The northern leaf-tailed gecko is the most familiar of them as well as being the largest. At a total length of over 12 inches (30 cm) it is Australia's longest gecko. Its closest rivals are the ring-tailed gecko, *Cyrtodactylus louisiadensis*, and the related chameleon gecko, *Carphodactylus laevis*, both of which have proportionately longer tails

Upside-Down Life

The northern leaf-tailed gecko is restricted to wet rain forests in the coastal ranges of northeastern Queensland, living mostly on the trunks of large forest trees and occasionally on saplings. Temperatures inside the forests are relatively low, but humidity is high. They lead vertical lives, resting on tree trunks with their head pointed downward.

During the day they remain motionless in the hollows formed by the pleated lower trunks of buttresses or in crevices and fissures in the bark. At night they begin to forage and work their way down the trunk until they are close to the bottom. They probably feed mainly on ground-dwelling insects that they ambush as they move close to the base of the tree. The

A New Genus

The genus *Saltuarius* was named in 1993 and contains five species. Prior to that all the Australian leaf-tailed geckos were placed in another genus, *Phyllurus*; some sources still refer to them by that name. *Phyllurus* contains eight species, six of them only described very recently. *Phyllurus platurus*, the southern leaf-tailed gecko, is common in the suburbs of Sydney, where it often enters houses and garages. It is smaller than the northern leaf-tailed gecko and has a broad but tapering tail. It inflates its body and gapes it mouth widely if it is attacked. Several species have very limited ranges in pockets of rain forest surrounded by drier habitats. *Phyllurus gulbaru*, described in 2003, for example, lives in an area of less than 9 square miles (23 sq. km) in northeastern Queensland.

geckos rarely travel across the ground, however. Other leaf-tailed geckos have similar feeding strategies, but some prefer to rest on the vertical faces of boulders.

The similarity between this species and the giant leaf-tailed geckos from Madagascar, *Uroplatus* species, is remarkable, even though they are in different families. The Australian species differs in having a more flattened shape, a spikier outline, and thinner limbs. Unlike the members of the Madagascan genus and most other geckos, its toes do not end in large adhesive pads but in claws. However, like the Madagascan species, its markings are equally effective at providing camouflage when it is resting on bark.

Reproduction in this species is poorly known, but related species mate in the fall (March), and females lay their eggs in midsummer (December and January), presumably having stored the sperm over the winter. Two soft-shelled eggs are laid, and the young hatch after about 60 days.

⊜ *It would be easy to miss this northern leaf-tailed gecko on a tree in Kuranda State Forest in Australia. Its extremely flat, leaf-shaped tail adds to the disguise.*

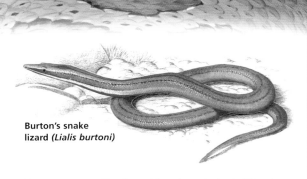

Burton's snake lizard *(Lialis burtoni)*

Common name Flap-footed lizards, scaly-footed lizards, snake lizards

Family Pygopodidae

Suborder Sauria

Order Squamata

Number of species 35

Size From 8 in (20 cm) to 30 in (76 cm) total length; average head and body length excluding tail from 3 in (7.6 cm) to 4.8 in (12 cm)

Key features Snakelike lizards with no visible limbs; some species have a small flap of skin in place of the hind legs; tail is at least as long as the head and body combined—often twice as long and occasionally 4 times as long—but regrown tails may be shorter; ear openings sometimes present; eyelids absent, and the lizards use their tongue to clean dust from their eyes

Habits Terrestrial and diurnal but secretive; often live in leaf litter

Breeding Egg layers; females produce 2 soft-shelled eggs; eggs hatch after 66–80 days in some species

Diet Insects, spiders, and scorpions; the snake lizards, *Lialis*, eat other lizards, especially skinks

Habitat Varied from open woodland and grassland to Mallee scrub and desert

Distribution Australia and southern New Guinea

Status Some species are extremely rare, possibly endangered; others can be fairly common in suitable habitat

Similar species None (other than snakes)

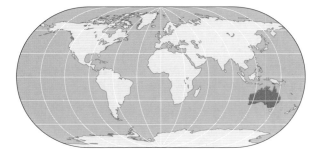

Flap-Footed Lizards

Pygopodidae

The flap-footed lizards are closely related to the geckos. These shy lizards stay out of sight most of the time, basking in upper layers of leaf litter and soil, and usually moving in the open only at night.

MEMBERS OF THE PYGOPODIDAE are known as flap-footed lizards or scaly-footed lizards. A few of them are also called snake lizards. There are 35 species altogether, and they are restricted to the Australasian region. With the exception of the extreme southeast, the rain forests of the east coast, and Tasmania, there is almost no part of Australia that does not have at least one or two species of flap-footed lizards. Burton's snake lizard, *Lialis burtoni*, is found over the widest area. It covers nearly all of Australia and part of New Guinea. The three species of *Pygopus* also cover most of Australia between them.

The closest relatives to the flap-footed lizards are the geckos in the family Diplodactylidae, and some scientists think that the Pygopodidae are types of gecko. The two families share certain characteristics, but these are mostly concerned with skulls and skeletons, and cannot be seen easily. One obvious similarity, however, is the lack of eyelids. Like geckos, flap-footed lizards cannot blink and therefore clean their eyes with their tongue.

Legless Lizards

Flap-footed lizards have no legs as such, but they have small scaly flaps on either side of the cloaca, where their hind legs would be if they had any. The front legs are missing altogether, but there is a pectoral girdle. The elongated tail indicates a terrestrial rather than a burrowing lifestyle. The tail is usually longer than the combined length of the head and body—in some species it can be twice the length of the head and body combined. Like geckos, flap-footed lizards shed their tail if grasped by a predator. They will eventually grow a new one

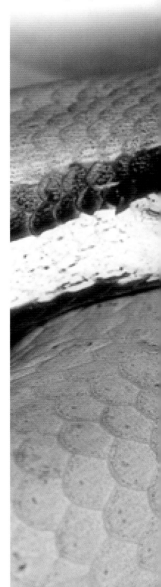

⊕ *Burton's snake lizard,* Lialis burtoni, *uses its tongue to clean its face and eyes. Living among soil, grass, or leaf litter and lacking eyelids, it has to do this to keep dust from covering its eyes.*

 SEE ALSO Geckos **45**:8; Snakes **48**:8

Burrowing Styles

Not all flap-footed lizards burrow, but many do. These species may push their way through friable (crumbly) soil, or they may occupy tunnels made by other animals, including ants and termites. The bronzeback, *Ophidiocephalus taeniatus,* bends its neck at an angle, using its head as a lever to pull the rest of its body and tail through the soil. The scaly-footed lizards belonging to the genus *Pygopus* have been seen excavating tunnels by picking up soil in their mouth to remove it. They also rotate, or spin, their body to enlarge the tunnel. Scientists think that this helps the lizards find and catch burrowing spiders, which are among their favorite foods.

that will be shorter than the original and may have different coloration.

Flap-footed lizards are covered with overlapping scales. In some species the scales have low keels running along the center. A few species also have keeled scales on the underside. Some species have external ear openings just behind the eyes, which immediately distinguishes them from snakes, but other species have no external ears, and parts of their internal ear structures may be missing too. Sound is obviously not an important aspect of their lives.

Secretive Lifestyles

None of the flap-footed lizards seems to have adapted to human activities. As a result, where land is developed for housing and farming, they tend to disappear. For this reason and because they are often hidden, the natural behavior of many species is not well known.

⊕ *Flap-footed lizards raise the head and front part of the body off the ground when hunting. The common scaly-foot,* Pygopus lepidopodus, *preys especially on scorpions and tunneling spiders.*

Most species eat insects and other invertebrates, such as spiders and scorpions, but a few of them (including the snake lizards, *Lialis*) eat larger prey such as other lizards and small birds and mammals. Some of these species have special adaptations to their teeth to help them overpower their prey.

Breeding habits are much the same among the various species and are similar to those of geckos. They normally lay two eggs at a time, although one or two species lay from one to three eggs.

Whereas most species are active in the day and bask in the sun, others are nocturnal or active at dusk. Whether they are active by night or by day depends on the climate. Flap-footed lizards from the hot interior of Australia are usually nocturnal, while species that live on the cooler coastal regions are active by day. Basking in the sun helps them raise their temperature and become more active. At extremely high temperatures they have to shelter from the heat, but flap-footed lizards can tolerate higher temperatures than many other lizards and only suffer from heat exhaustion if the temperature rises above 104°F (40°C) or even 111°F (44°C).

Varied Habitat

The different species of flap-footed lizards occupy a wide variety of habitats, including desert, grassland, and woodland. They live on the ground or burrow under loose sand or soil, or hide beneath leaf litter, rocks, logs, or dense vegetation. There are no climbing species. Depending on where they come from, they may shelter in clumps or hummocks of spinifex or porcupine grass that grow in dry places. Or they may hide under logs and stones that are partially buried in the ground. Species that come from wooded areas usually live among the dead leaves that collect on the ground or in hollows, including dried-up streambeds. One species, *Paradelma orientalis,* occasionally climbs up the bark of eucalyptus trees. This may enable it to look for prey over a wider area.

A few species of *Delma* and *Aprasia* and the bronzeback, *Ophidiocephalus taeniatus* (which is the only member of its genus), are usually found only below the surface. These burrowing species usually live in places where the soil is sandy and loose so they can easily push their way through it. They are hard to find, and some of them have been collected only on a few occasions. Those that live where the soil is harder do not burrow. Instead, they make use of the burrows made by other small animals when they need to hide or shelter from extreme heat or cold. *Aprasia* species live in termite mounds and ant tunnels.

Foraging at Ground Level

Flap-footed lizards are mostly opportunistic foragers, searching for their food in the course of their daily movements. When they are hunting, they frequently raise their head and the front part of their body off the ground to get a better view of their surroundings. They also use their forked tongue in the same way as snakes to "taste" their surroundings. The tongue picks up scent particles and transfers them to the Jacobson's organ. Even so, the lizards can also use their tongue to help swallow food, unlike snakes, in which the tongue is not suitable for this purpose.

These species do not appear to specialize in any particular prey, although the common scaly-foot, *Pygopus lepidopodus*, eats more scorpions than other species and also eats large tunneling

Classification

Despite their appearance, flap-footed lizards are related to geckos. Their closest relatives are those in the family Diplodactylidae, also largely Australian, but with some species in New Zealand and neighboring islands. Flap-footed lizards share certain important characteristics with those of diplodactylid and typical geckos in the family Gekkonidae, notably their lack of eyelids. Some scientists think that the flap-footed lizards should be included within the Diplodactylidae.

Snake Mimics

There are several instances of mimicry among snakes: The harmless American milksnakes, *Lampropeltis triangulum*, that look like venomous coral snakes are a good example. Lizards cannot normally use this trick because most of them have legs. Flap-footed lizards, however, have an advantage here, and at least one species, the black-headed scaly-foot, *Pygopus nigriceps*, has grown to look very similar to several species of small, black-headed snakes belonging to the cobra family. If it is threatened, it lifts its head off the ground and flattens its neck, just like one of the cobras.

 *More than any other flap-footed lizard, the black-headed scaly-foot,* Pygopus nigriceps, *resembles a true snake, and this mimicry gives it a degree of protection.*

spiders. When tackling prey that could fight back and cause injuries, the lizard grasps it in its jaws and spins rapidly to break it into pieces. All the species that feed on insects and other invertebrates have typical lizard teeth: blunt and rounded and firmly attached to the jawbones. Their main purpose is to crush the prey so that it is easier to swallow.

Tail Lurers

A couple of species eat larger prey such as small snakes and other lizards. They are the strange snake lizards belonging to the genus *Lialis* that occur throughout Australia and in New Guinea. These species ambush their prey by hiding in a clump of tussock grass, for example, then attacking with a sudden rush.

In order to increase the chances of a small lizard coming within range, they hide their head and body but hold their tail in a conspicuous position. When a lizard comes into view, they wiggle the tip of their tail to imitate the actions of a small worm or caterpillar. When the lizard comes closer to investigate, the snake lizard strikes. Tail luring occurs only in a few species of snakes (although they are widespread and from a number of different families) but has not been recorded in any other lizards.

Because of their unusual diet the snake lizards, *Lialis,* have several specialized features. Their jaws are very long, resulting in a narrow, pointed snout. The jawbones are very flexible, and the lizard can bend the tip of its upper jaw down to touch the tip of its lower jaw even when it is holding a large prey item. It uses its jaws like a pair of pincers, making sure that the prey cannot wriggle away. The teeth are curved and pointed, more like the teeth of snakes than other lizards. Instead of being fixed firmly to the jaw, they are only loosely attached with cartilage. This allows them to fold back, which is very useful when holding onto plump, smooth-scaled lizards such as skinks.

Reproduction

The breeding habits of flap-footed lizards are not well known. Like the geckos, these lizards have a voice. Although they use it to make a high-pitched squeak (when they are picked up, for example), species with hearing apparatus may use it for communication as well.

Flap-footed lizards are not normally social animals. They are usually found singly, but occasionally small groups have been found together under a stone, for instance. It is likely that they have come together for breeding, but more observations of this kind will be necessary before firm conclusions can be drawn.

The species that live in the cooler parts of Australia all mate in spring and lay their eggs in summer. No one knows if they breed once or several times during a single year. Species that live in more tropical parts probably breed at any time of the year, although they may react to dry or wet seasons—again, there is just not enough information to be sure about this.

Most of the species that have been studied lay two eggs, although *Lialis* sometimes lay one or three eggs instead of the usual two. Flap-footed lizards' eggs are elongated, and the shells are rubbery like those of diplodactylid and eublepharid geckos. Females of some species belonging to the genera *Pygopus* and *Lialis* may lay their eggs together in communal breeding sites. Unfortunately, flap-footed lizards' eggs are rarely found. In the few species that have been studied, the eggs take from 66 to 80 days to hatch, and the newly hatched babies are similar in appearance to their parents.

Habitat Destruction

Although some species of flap-footed lizards (such as Burton's snake lizard, *Lialis burtoni)* are doing well and occur over a wide area, several other species are suffering as a result of habitat loss caused by replanting, building, or clearance for crops. The most affected species are those that live in specialized grassland habitats. Before Europeans settled in this part of the world, the natural habitat consisted of vast, treeless plains covered with grasses such as kangaroo grass and spear grass. The grasses grow in tussocks, and this characteristic seems to be important to the flap-footed lizards, possibly because they hibernate in the bases of the clumps.

Since settlement by Europeans, however, most of the grassland has been altered. Planting with other species of grasses for stock grazing has occurred over most of the lizards' former ranges. The new grasses do not form the tussocks that the lizards need, and in any case they

⊕ *The specialized grassland habitats of the spinifex snake lizard,* Delma nasuta, *are under threat, and the species is protected in some areas of Australia, including the Northern Territory.*

are heavily grazed by cattle. Another habitat that has been affected is known as Mallee scrub, which is a kind of heathland with low-growing bushes and sandy soil. Much of this habitat has been burned off so that the land can be used for farming or building.

As a result, a number of species do not occur over as large an area as they used to. One is the striped flap-footed lizard, *Delma impar*, an inhabitant of the old tussock grasslands, and another is the Mallee worm lizard, *Aprasia aurita*, which lives in Mallee scrub. Both species come from the southeastern corner of Australia mainly in the state of Victoria, and the striped flap-footed lizard also reaches small areas of the neighbouring states of New South Wales and South Australia.

Habitat destruction has not only reduced the number of suitable places in which these species can live, it has also fragmented what is left into small pieces separated by roads, towns, and farms. Fires started by humans have spoiled much of the habitat and probably killed large numbers of the lizards as well.

Rescue Plans

Steps are being taken to try to save the two species that are in trouble before they become extinct. Several other species will face exactly the same crisis if they happen to live in this type of landscape, where human activity and the lizards' requirements are in conflict.

There is only a limited amount that can be done to help the flap-footed lizards. Once their habitat is gone, it is difficult or even impossible to return it to its original state. So the various conservation authorities are concentrating on several "damage-limitation" programs. The most important is to set up nature reserves in places where the original habitat has not been too badly affected in order to stop further destruction. Then the lizards living in the reserves need to be studied to see if any other types of management, such as scrub clearance, would benefit them. Any lizards that are found away from the reserves (on roads, for instance) can be caught and used for two more purposes. First, they can be exhibited to the general public so that they know what the lizards look like and will therefore be more likely to take an interest in them. As a last resort, animals taken from unsuitable places can be used for captive-breeding programs in the hope that they can be released back into a nature reserve at a later date and added to the numbers already there.

Leaping to Their Own Defense

Flap-footed lizards are more or less defenseless and are eaten by a number of different predators, including hawks, snakes, monitor lizards, and domestic cats. Some of them use cunning methods to avoid predation. For example, the species with particularly long tails, namely the 16 *Delma* species and *Pletholax gracilis*, attempt to escape by leaping into the air. They use their long tail like a coiled spring to launch themselves up, a tactic that is designed to confuse and startle predators.

Night Lizards

The Xantusiidae, usually known as the night lizards, is a small family of three genera and 26 species. Its members are restricted to the Americas, with one genus (consisting of a single species) from Cuba. The largest genus, *Lepidophyma*, has 19 species occurring throughout Central America from Mexico to Panama. In the genus *Xantusia* one species, the island night lizard, *X. riversiana*, is found only on the Channel Islands off southern California, and the remaining five *Xantusia* species are found in western North America from Utah and Nevada to Baja California and Durango, Mexico.

Most night lizards are small, although *X. riversiana* grows to about 7 inches (18 cm) long, and some of the Central American species exceed this slightly. In many ways the members of this family are like geckos. They lack movable eyelids and use their tongue to wipe their eyes clean. The back is covered with small granular scales.

In the Central American night lizards, *Lepidophyma*, the small scales are interspersed with irregular large, tubercular scales that sometimes gives them a slightly "prickly" appearance (*Lepidophyma* means "warty scales"). On the underside the scales are rectangular in shape and arranged in regular rows touching each other but not overlapping. In addition, the scales covering the top of the head are large, platelike, and arranged symmetrically.

Body shape can be cylindrical, but several species are flattened from top to bottom so that they can fit into narrow crevices—there can even be variation within a species if different populations have different habits. All species have four limbs, although they are small in the Cuban night lizard, *Cricosaura typica*, which moves in a snakelike manner. The tail in night lizards is relatively short, as in most geckos, but they have no toe pads.

Primitive Placenta

All species are viviparous (live-bearing), and the females provide the developing embryos with nourishment through a primitive type of placenta. Clutch sizes are small—one to four young in each clutch is typical, and growth rates after birth are slow. Nevertheless, the island night lizard, *X. riversiana*, occurs in densities of up to 1,300 per 1 acre (0.4 ha), and this large species can produce broods of up to nine young. The low reproductive potential of night lizards in general indicates that individuals live for a long time. This seems to be borne out by their behavior in captivity, where they prefer

---

Common name Night lizards **Family** Xantusiidae

Family Xantusiidae 3 genera and 26 species:
  Genus *Cricosaura*—1 species from Cuba, *C. typica*
  Genus *Lepidophyma*—19 species of Central American night lizards, including the yellow-spotted night lizard, *L. flavimaculatum*
  Genus *Xantusia*—6 species of night lizards from North and Central America, including the granite night lizard, *X. henshawi*, and the desert night lizard, *X. vigilis*

 SEE ALSO Lizards **44**:8; Geckos **45**:8; Lizard, Granite Night **45**:56

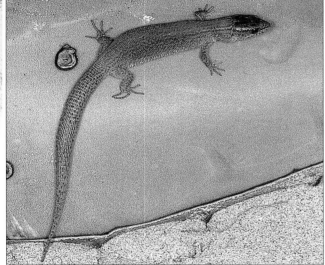

⊙ *Members of the genus* Lepidophyma *are distributed from Mexico to Panama. This is the Mexican night lizard,* Lepidophyma pajapanensis.

common species, and more is known about its reproduction than that of most other species. Females give birth to between four and six live young in the rainy season that lasts from May to November. Unusually, the births can be spread over two to three days. The young are relatively large at birth but grow slowly, taking 20 months to reach maturity. A related species, *L. reticulatus* (also from Costa Rica), may also be parthenogenetic, since only females have been collected so far. However, this species is rare, and males may still be discovered.

Insect Eaters

Like most small lizards, night lizards are mainly insectivorous in their feeding habits, eating invertebrates ranging from ants to beetles and cockroaches depending on their size. The island night lizard, however, is omnivorous and will also eat flowers and seeds. Smith's tropical night lizard, *L. smithii* from southern Mexico, Guatemala, and El Salvador, eats mainly figs that fall into the caves where it lives.

Activity patterns of the "night" lizards are not as straightforward as their name implies. In fact, most species are apparently active in the day. But because they live in crevices or among leaf litter and often in dark, secluded places, their activities go unnoticed. Some species tend to emerge from their hiding places after dark or at dusk, and this gives the impression that they are strictly nocturnal. From what little we know about them, it seems that night lizards are not adventurous, and many individuals apparently spend their entire lives in a small area, perhaps under a single log or rock! Having said that, their activity patterns can change according to the conditions. The Cuban night lizard may be quite common in leaf litter in the wet season but hard or impossible to find in the same places during the dry season, when it retreats into places that retain some moisture.

⊙ *The desert night lizard,* Xantusia vigilis, *is found in association with plants such as yucca, digger pine, and juniper. It is a secretive lizard, spending most of its time in and under yucca logs and other cover.*

low temperatures, they move slowly and deliberately, they eat very little, and they grow slowly.

Some populations of the yellow-spotted night lizard, *Lepidophyma flavimaculatum*, consist of females only and are presumed to reproduce parthenogenetically. All-female populations live in Panama and throughout most of Costa Rica. In northern Costa Rica and in Honduras, however, populations contain males in small numbers. These populations probably reproduce sexually. It is a

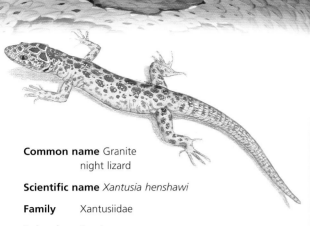

Common name Granite
night lizard

Scientific name *Xantusia henshawi*

Family Xantusiidae

Suborder Sauria

Order Squamata

Size From 4 in (10 cm) to 5 in (13 cm) long

Key features A small, flattened lizard with smooth, shiny
skin made up of a large number of small
scales; eyes moderately large with vertical
pupils but no movable eyelids; head wide and
flattened and covered with large, symmetrical
scales; markings consist of large dark-brown
blotches separated by narrow white or yellow
netting; limbs thin with long claws for
climbing

Habits Very secretive; active in the evening

Breeding Female gives birth to 1–2 young in the fall;
gestation period about 3 months

Diet Small invertebrates and some plant material

Habitat Rocky outcrops and hillsides in canyons,
where it hides in crevices

Distribution Southern California and northern Baja
California, Mexico

Status Common in suitable habitat

Similar species *Xantusia bezyi*, recently described from
Arizona, is very similar, as is *X. bolsonae* from
Durango, Mexico

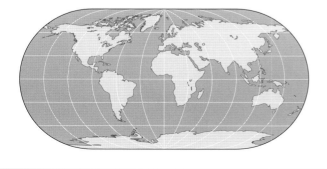

LIZARDS

Granite Night Lizard

Xantusia henshawi

*The granite night lizard is easily overlooked, since it
lives in crevices in massive rocks and boulders. It
rarely ventures out in the open until after dark.*

RECENTLY HERPETOLOGISTS HAVE QUESTIONED the term
"night" lizard, especially in relation to the
granite night lizards, because they are probably
active during the day. However, the activity
takes place deep in crevices in large boulders,
where they cannot be seen.

Granite night lizards are colonial lizards
living in quite small areas of suitable habitat.
They often live on granite rocks in canyons and
gullies, where they are protected from direct
sunlight for part of the day, and where a little
humidity remains well into the summer.

Because the granite night lizard has such a
specialized habitat, its occurrence is patchy even
within the small area over which it occurs, and
there are large gaps in its distribution. Some
populations differ superficially from others, and
several subspecies have been described. One
form discovered in Arizona was originally
considered to be a variation of the desert night
lizard, *X. vigilis*. But its markings are similar to
those of the granite night lizard, and in 2001 it
was described as a separate species, *X. bezyi*.

Spring Breeding

Male granite night lizards have a small gland on
the inside of their thighs as well as a row of
femoral pores. These pores probably produce
substances that allow the males to mark their
territories, although little is known about
communications or social interactions.

Breeding takes place in spring, and the
female gives birth to one or two young in the
fall after a gestation of about three months.
The young take two or more years to reach
maturity. This is unusual for a small lizard, most
of which grow rapidly and breed quickly.
For example, the side-blotched lizard,

Predators are limited to larger lizards, snakes, and predatory birds. In recent times their biggest threat has come from people collecting them for the pet trade and for research.

The only way of catching them is to pry off the large flakes of rock under which they shelter. This causes permanent damage to the habitat, since there are only a limited number of rock flakes for them to live under, and tens of thousands of years will have to pass before the weathering process will produce more flakes. Many areas have been badly damaged in the past by collectors, and the species is now protected not because it is particularly rare, but because the collecting method is so destructive.

As its name suggests, the granite night lizard can usually be found under pieces of flaking granite in rocky areas of southern California and Mexico.

Uta stansburiana, which comes from the same part of the world but belongs to the Iguanidae, is practically "annual," with almost a complete turnover of individuals between one breeding season and the next.

Threats

The survival rate of the young is thought to be very high because they rarely stray from the crevices in which they live, even at night.

Close Relatives

The desert night lizard, *Xantusia vigilis* from North America, is smaller than the granite night lizard and more widespread. It is not quite as specialized in its habitat requirements and lives in small colonies among rocks or between the overlapping leaves in the bases of live and dead yucca plants. Interestingly, colonies living in yucca debris have cylindrical bodies, whereas those living among rocks have flattened bodies like that of the granite night lizard.

The island night lizard, *X. riversiana*, is just like a desert night lizard but several times bigger. This species is restricted to three small islands off the coast of southern California, where it has federal protection. Because insect food is hard to come by, this species has adopted an omnivorous diet and eats the flowers and seeds of succulent plants and annuals that grow on the islands. Two Mexican species, *X. bolsonae* from Durango and *X. sanchezi* (described in 1999 from Zacatecas, Mexico), are poorly known.

Wall Lizards

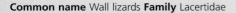

The lacertids are variously known as wall lizards, sand lizards, Old World lizards, or "true" lizards, none of which are very satisfactory names. There are about 279 species in 26 genera, and they occur in Europe, Africa, Central and Southeast Asia, Taiwan, and Japan. There are no universally accepted subfamilies.

Lacertids are mostly medium-sized lizards, although a few, such as the eyed, or jeweled, lizard, *Lacerta lepida*, the Canary Island lizards, *Gallotia*, and the African *Nucras* species are quite large, growing to over 2 feet (60 cm) long including the tail. Typically they have cylindrical or slightly flattened bodies, movable eyelids, long limbs, and a long tail. The scales on their back are small and beadlike, while those on the underside are rectangular

and arranged in rows. The head is covered with large, platelike scales. Although many species are well camouflaged, others are bright and showy, especially many of the European *Podarcis* and *Lacerta* species, in which the dominant males are often brilliantly colored during the breeding season. Other species change color and markings as they grow and mature. Some of the small wall lizards from Mediterranean islands, notably the Balearics, have stunning shades of bright green and blue; others have all-black, melanistic colonies on small offshore islands.

Habitat Types

Lacertids are mostly terrestrial or rock climbers. They are agile sun worshipers, basking conspicuously but quick to dart away if approached. They soon reemerge, however, often a few feet from where they were first seen. In southern Europe and North Africa they often live near humans and are a common sight climbing over stone walls surrounding fields, buildings, ancient ruins, and in villages and on the edges of towns. Some species are hardly ever seen away from human habitations. Many live on Mediterranean islands, where each group of islands often has an endemic species or subspecies. The Canary Islands off the west coast of Africa also have endemic species, some of which are very rare.

Desert species have a number of adaptations. Several species, such as *Acanthodactylus* in southern Europe and North Africa and *Meroles* in southern Africa, have fringes on their toes to help them run across loose sand. *Meroles* species from the Namib Desert are "sand swimmers," diving into loose sand to escape from predators and to avoid the worst of the midday heat.

A few lacertids are arboreal, notably the beautiful African blue-tailed tree lizard, *Holaspis guentheri*. It has a

---

Common name Wall lizards **Family** Lacertidae

Family Lacertidae 26 genera, about 279 species. Important genera include:

Genus *Acanthodactylus*—38 species of fringe-toed, or fingered, lizards from Europe, Africa, the Middle East, and India, including the fringe-toed lizard, *A. erythrurus*

Genus *Darevskia*—22 species (some parthenogenetic) from the Caucasus region, including the Russian rock lizard, *D. saxicola*

Genus *Gallotia*—7 species of Canary Island lizards, including the Gran Canaria giant lizard, *G. stehlini*, and the La Gomera giant lizard, *G. gomerana*

Genus *Holaspis*—2 species of African tree lizards, including the blue-tailed tree lizard, *H. guentheri*

Genus *Heliobolus*—4 species, including the bushveld lizard, *H. lugubris* from southern Africa

Genus *Lacerta*—38 species of green, eyed, viviparous lizards from Europe, North Africa, and the Middle East, including the Iberian rock lizard, *L. monticola*, Schreiber's lizard, *L. schreiberi*, the eyed (or jeweled) lizard, *L. lepida*, the green lizard, *L. viridis*, the viviparous lizard, *L. vivipara*

Genus *Meroles*—7 desert lizards from Africa

Genus *Nucras*—8 sandveld lizards from Africa, including the western sandveld lizard, *N. tessellata*

Genus *Ophisops*—8 species without a collective common name from Asia and eastern Europe, including the snake-eyed lizard, *O. elegans*

Genus *Podarcis*—18 species of wall lizards from southern Europe and western Asia, including Lilford's wall lizard, *P. lilfordi*, the common wall lizard, *P. muralis*, the Ibiza wall lizard, *P. pityusensis*, the Italian wall lizard, *P. sicula*

Genus *Psammodromus*—4 species of sand racers from southwestern Europe and North Africa, including the large sand racer, *P. algirus*

Genus *Takydromus*—18 species of grass lizards or long-tailed lizards from Asia, including the six-lined grass lizard, *T. sexlineatus*

 SEE ALSO Lizard, Bushveld **45:**62; Lizard, Eyed **45:**64; Lizard, Viviparous **45:**68; Lizards, African Desert and Sand **45:**74

⊕ *Lacertids have small beadlike scales on their back and large platelike scales on the head. The ornate sandveld lizard,* Nucras ornata *from Africa, is one of the larger species and can grow to 27 inches (70 cm).*

flattened body and a fringe of backward-pointing, tooth-shaped scales down each side of its tail. It uses the scales to grip rough tree bark as it climbs. More unusually, it can jump from one tree to another, gliding considerable distances with the aid of its flattened tail, which acts like a parachute. Other arboreal species include at least two of the African keel-bellied lizards, *Gastropholis*—*G. echinata* and *G. prasina*. They live in tree holes and move around in the branches using their prehensile tails. Both are bright green in color.

Three of the four species of forest lizards, *Adolfus* from East Africa, climb fallen and standing tree trunks in montane forests, although one

⊖ *A European species,* Podarcis muralis, *the common wall lizard, has attractive brown mottled markings. It is often seen basking vertically on walls close to towns.*

species, the alpine meadow lizard, *A. alleni*, lives in a habitat that is devoid of trees and therefore does not climb. It lives in moorland between 8,800 and 14,750 feet (2,680–4,500 m) in the Aberdare Mountains and Mount Elgon, Kenya, and is the highest-occurring lacertid. It is also probably the highest-occurring lizard in Africa.

The grass lizards, *Takydromus* from Asia, also climb, but they restrict their activities to tall grass stems. They are extremely elongated, with a tail that can be four times the length of the head and body combined. When moving rapidly, they "swim" through vegetation, changing direction quickly and at random, making it difficult to follow their movements.

With the exception of the sand-swimming desert lizards, there are no burrowing species. But several, such as the sand lizards, *Pedioplanis* from Africa, dig short burrows under rocks in which they shelter at night.

Evasion Tactics

Lacertids are quick, alert lizards that rely mostly on speed and agility to escape from predators, of which there are many, including larger lizards, snakes, birds,

and small carnivorous mammals. In parts of southern Europe domestic cats probably kill more wall lizards than any other predator. The lizards can also discard their tails, which continue to wriggle and attract the attention of predators while the rest of the lizard escapes. A few species, such as the Anatolian wall lizard, *Lacerta anatolica*, and juvenile Iberian rock lizards, *L. monticola*, have brightly colored tails—often blue—to direct the attacks of predators to that part of their anatomy.

Others have more sophisticated methods of deterring predators. Young bushveld lizards, *Heliobolus lugubris*, mimic noxious beetles both in their markings and their behavior. The African blue-tailed tree lizard, *Holaspis guentheri*, sleeps with its body concealed but its brightly colored tail coiled up like a clock spring, perhaps in an attempt to imitate an armored millipede.

Diverse Diet

Most lacertids feed opportunistically on any small insects they find. Several switch diets according to the food available to them. For example, they may eat small beetles for part of the year then move to ants or termites if they become common. In northern Spain the Iberian rock lizards, *L. monticola*, live near glacial lakes. They feed heavily on newly emerged damselflies and mayflies when they are hatching in large numbers in the summer. In Namibia the shovel-snouted lizard, *Meroles anchietae*, eats windblown seeds of grasses and desert plants by waiting in the hollows between dunes, where seeds accumulate during windy weather. If the wind dies down, it goes off in search of insects.

Larger species and some of the smaller ones eat plant material as well as insects. The large eyed, or jeweled, lizard, *L. lepida*, eats fruit if other prey is in short supply; otherwise it eats insects, smaller lizards, and other vertebrates. Some of the species living on barren Mediterranean islands, such as Lilford's wall lizard, *Podarcis lilfordi*, eat varying amounts of vegetable material depending on where they live. Some populations of this species living on small offshore islands feed almost entirely on the fruit, flowers, nectar, and pollen of succulent, salt-tolerant plants that rely in turn on the

Spectacles and Goggles

Although lacertids typically have movable eyelids, the snake-eyed lizard, *Ophisops elegans* from Eastern Europe, parts of the Middle East, and North Africa, has a transparent spectacle covering its eye and no eyelids, so it cannot blink. Whereas geckos and night lizards use their tongue to wipe the spectacle clean, the snake-eyed lizard pulls the spectacle briefly downward to wipe any dust or grains of sand against the upper edge of the scale bordering the bottom of the eye (the suborbital scale). It uses the muscles that would otherwise operate the lower eyelid. The Moroccan rock lizard, *Lacerta perspicillata* from North Africa, has a transparent window in its lower eyelid so that it can see even when it closes its eyelids, as if it were wearing goggles. This is probably an adaptation to living in places where sandstorms can be a problem.

⊕ *The Vedrá Island wall lizard,* **Podarcis pityusensis vedrae,** *is a colorful subspecies of Iberian wall lizard that occurs only on the tiny islet of Vedrá off Ibiza in the Mediterranean.*

lizards for pollination. Members of the same species also scavenge around the nests of seabird colonies, taking pieces of spilled fish and the flies they attract. Lilford's wall lizard also feeds on scraps of discarded prey from around the nests of Eleonora's falcon, *Falco eleonorae*. Two other Mediterranean wall lizards, Erhard's wall lizard, *Podarcis erhardii*, and the Skyros wall lizard, *P. gaigeae*, do exactly the same thing on the Greek islands of Crete and the Diabates Islands west of Skyros respectively.

Reproduction

With a single exception—the viviparous lizard, *Lacerta vivipara*—lacertids lay eggs. They often have complicated social lives, with brightly colored males defending a territory containing several females. The bright colors of the males are often intensified in the breeding season, and they use substances secreted by pores on their thighs to mark their territory. Subordinate males have more subdued coloration to avoid conflict, but fights break out when two males are equally matched. Fighting animals inflate their throats and circle one another while angling their bodies to make themselves look as large as possible. If this display is not sufficient to send the trespasser running for cover, the conflict is stepped up, and each lizard tries to bite the other. Broken tails are a common result of these fights.

Mating usually takes place in the spring, although the breeding habits of tropical and subtropical species are poorly known and may be less seasonal. Females lay clutches of four to 10 soft-shelled eggs (up to 20 in some of the larger species) in short burrows often dug under rocks. They hatch after about 30 to 45 days. Females may lay more than one clutch in a year. The Milos wall lizard, *Podarcis milensis*, is different. Females lay many small clutches of one to three eggs throughout the summer.

Some of the rough-scaled lizards, *Ichnotropis* from southern and Central Africa, are "annuals." In other words, they mature in five to eight months, lay one or two clutches of eggs, then die before the next generation matures. Two such species, the Cape rough-scaled lizard, *I. capensis*, and the common rough-scaled lizard, *I. squamulosa*, whose habitat overlaps for much of their range, stagger their reproductive cycles so that the juveniles hatch at different times and do not compete.

Five lacertids from the Caucasus region can reproduce without males—they are parthenogenetic. This fact was discovered in 1958, and *L. saxatilis* (later renamed *Darevskia saxatilis*) was the first-known parthenogenetic lizard. Others followed—parthenogenesis is now known in several lizard families, including Teiidae and Gekkonidae.

Common name Bushveld lizard

Scientific name *Heliobolus lugubris*

Family Lacertidae

Suborder Sauria

Order Squamata

Size 6 in (15 cm) long

Key features Typically lacertid in shape with a pointed snout, cylindrical body, and long limbs and tail; adults are light grayish brown or reddish brown in color with 3 pale cream stripes running down the back; only the center stripe continues onto the tail, which is brown; juveniles are completely different, black with white spots and a sandy-colored tail

Habits Terrestrial and diurnal

Breeding Female lays clutch of 4–6 eggs; eggs hatch after about 6 weeks

Diet Small insects, especially termites

Habitat Dry grassland and scrub

Distribution Southern Africa

Status Common in suitable habitat

Similar species The many African desert lacertids can be difficult to identify in the field; the bold stripes of this species are a good field mark, and juveniles are very distinctive; 2 other species in the genus occur farther north in East Africa; another occurs in West and Central Africa

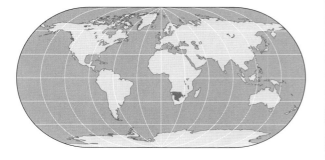

Bushveld Lizard

Heliobolus lugubris

Adult bushveld lizards live typical lacertid lives, darting from bush to bush in dry, sandy grasslands and hunting small insects. The juveniles, however, have an unusual strategy for defending themselves.

ADULT BUSHVELD LIZARDS ARE BASICALLY sandy colored to match the surface on which they live. In contrast, the hatchlings' bodies are black with white spots. Their tails, however, match the sand. As a result, the young lizards appear to have no tail. Their black-and-white body markings imitate those of noxious oogpister beetles from the region. *Oogpister* means "eye squirter" in Afrikaans—the beetles spray an acidic substance into the eyes of any animal rash enough to molest them. As a result, birds and small mammalian predators avoid them.

Beetle Mimics

As well as looking like the beetles, the young lizards behave like them, walking in a jerky manner on stiff legs. They arch their back to resemble the beetles' wing cases and keep their tail flat on the ground. Oogpister beetles grow only to about 2 inches (5 cm) long, however, so this deception has a limited life. Remarkably, as they approach that size, the lizards' markings gradually change to the adults' camouflage colors.

Does this unusual defensive strategy work? Scientists have found that juvenile bushveld lizards are less likely to have broken or regrown tails than other lacertid lizards from the same region, which would indicate that predators avoid them.

As far as anyone knows, juvenile bushveld lizards are the only ones

⬀ *The simple trick of having a camouflaged tail enables juvenile bushveld lizards to be mistaken for poisonous beetles. Predators therefore tend to leave them alone.*

to imitate beetles; but the young of a South American galliwasp lizard, *Diploglossus lessonae*, are marked with bold black-and-white bands (even though the adults are brown). The juveniles apparently mimic a brightly colored millipede, *Rhinocricus albidolimbatus*, that produces nasty chemicals. Galliwasp lizards are elongated; once again, the lizard moves in the same way as the millipede, and the mimicry is very convincing. Both millipedes and hatchling lizards appear during the rainy season, but the millipedes gradually disappear as the dry season approaches; at the same time, the lizards' markings begin to fade into those of the adults.

Other examples of lizards mimicking invertebrates include the banded geckos, *Coleonyx*, and the leopard geckos, *Eublepharis*. They have banded tails, especially as juveniles, that they hold above the body when moving, in apparent imitation of scorpions. There are probably many other examples that have not yet come to light.

Typical Lifestyle

Leaving aside the beetle-mimicking antics of the juveniles, the bushveld lizard's lifestyle is typical of African lacertids. It feeds mainly on termites and other small insects, dashing from the cover of one bush to another to avoid extremes

African Relatives

Three other species of *Heliobolus* live farther north in Africa but are poorly known. It is unlikely that their juveniles are beetle mimics because the oogpister beetles do not occur in the region. Sandveld lizards, genus *Nucras*, occur over much the same area but appear to prefer sandier places and are very secretive and difficult to observe. Unlike the bushveld lizards that tend to wait under cover for prey to appear, the sandveld lizards are active foragers, poking around in nooks and crannies for insects. The western sandveld lizard, *Nucras tessellata*, which is beautifully marked with vertical white bars on its dark gray or black body and reddish-brown hind limbs and tail, is a specialized hunter of scorpions and spiders. It digs them out of their burrows, and it also takes other insects.

of heat and the attentions of predators. Females lay between four and six soft-shelled eggs in a small burrow that they excavate in loose sandy soil. They probably lay two or more clutches throughout the summer, but information is lacking. Hatchlings are about from December to March, and the likely incubation period is roughly six weeks. After March the juveniles and adults enter a short period of hibernation.

Common name Eyed lizard (jeweled lizard, jeweled lacerta, ocellated lizard)

Scientific name *Lacerta lepida*

Family Lacertidae

Suborder Sauria

Order Squamata

Size From 24 in (60 cm) to 30 in (76 cm)

Key features A large lizard with a massive head, especially in males; body only slightly flattened; tail thick at the base; usually green on the back with black stippling and a number of blue spots, or ocelli, on the sides; females are more brownish green than males and have fewer blue spots; spots may be absent altogether

Habits Terrestrial and diurnal

Breeding Female lays 4–6 eggs that hatch in 8–14 weeks; occasionally lays a second clutch

Diet Almost anything; large insects, other lizards, snakes, frogs, rodents, and nestling birds; also fruit and other vegetation

Habitat Varied but usually dry hillsides, scrub, roadsides, olive groves, vineyards

Distribution Iberian Peninsula, southern France, and extreme northwestern Italy

Status Common but never in high densities

Similar species Green lizards, including *L. viridis*, and Schreiber's lizard, *L. schreiberi*, are sometimes similar to small eyed lizards, but they all lack the blue eyespots

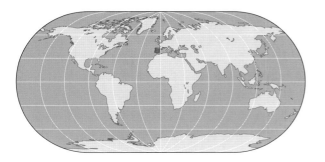

Eyed Lizard

Lacerta lepida

Apart from the very elongated legless lizard, Ophisaurus apodus *in the family Anguidae, the eyed lizard is the largest lizard in Europe and by far the most impressive to look at.*

THE EYED LIZARD IS A POWERFUL SPECIES with a large head and strong jaws. It easily crushes the shells of large beetles and can also tackle small vertebrates such as mice, voles, and birds with no trouble. It will even take baby rabbits. When cornered by a predator or a human, it opens its mouth widely and hisses, sometimes jumping forward in a threatening manner. If it is picked up, it bites very hard, and even a half-grown individual can easily draw blood.

Despite this, the eyed lizard is normally a timid species, making off at great speed at the slightest disturbance. If it happens to be living near scrub or dry vegetation, the first sign of its presence is the noisy crashing of undergrowth as it runs away (despite its scientific name *lepida,* meaning graceful). It hides in a burrow, under a large rock, or in cavities in drystone walls or rock piles and is very hard to dislodge once it has gone to ground.

By the time it has reached adult size, it has few predators except larger carnivorous mammals, such as foxes and weasels, and the larger birds of prey. None of the snakes in the region are big enough even to consider eating an adult eyed lizard—in fact, the opposite is more likely to happen.

Social Behavior

Male eyed lizards are very territorial and often take up basking positions on top of prominent boulders or logs, from where they can watch for intruders as well as predators. Well-matched males may fight, circling each other with their

⊖ *The eyed lizard is the largest of all lacertid species and can reach up to 30 inches (76 cm) long. Females and juveniles are missing the distinctive blue eyespots.*

throats inflated and making sudden darts to try to bite their opponent while it is offguard. Territory holders mate with any females that live in their territory.

The gestation period is much longer than it is in smaller lacertids, and females lay their eggs about 10 to 14 weeks after mating. Clutch size is large, with up to 22 eggs recorded. However, smaller clutches are laid by females in less favorable habitats, especially dry and barren places. The eggs are usually laid in a chamber in damp soil or leaf litter under a rock or log. In southern parts of the range, where their active

⊕ *Schreiber's lizard,* Lacerta schreiberi, *is similar to the eyed lizard. It is found in the Iberian peninsula, where it lives mainly in moist, hilly areas.*

Spanish Relatives

Although there are a number of large lacertids, only two come into contact with the eyed lizard. The green lizard, *L. viridis*, lives alongside it in southern France and the extreme northeast of Spain. Its preferred habitats and its habits are much the same as those of the eyelid lizard, although it tends to live in discrete colonies with higher population densities.

Schreiber's lizard (sometimes known as the Spanish eyed lizard), *L. schreiberi*, occurs in the Iberian Peninsula but is restricted mainly to higher elevations than the eyed lizard. Schreiber's lizards are rarely, if ever, found together with eyed lizards. They are associated with more humid conditions and often live alongside mountain streams and rivers. They are prepared to dive into the water to escape enemies. In other places, such as the Sierra de Gredos, they live above the tree line in rocky, moorland habitat. Male Schreiber's lizards are similar to eyed lizards, but they are smaller and lack the blue eyespots. They often have a blue throat and sometimes a blue head too, especially in the breeding season. Females are completely different—they are brown or bright green with large black spots down the middle of the back and on their flanks.

period is longer, females may lay a second clutch, but one is more usual. The eggs take eight to 14 weeks to hatch.

The total length of the hatchlings is about 4.5 to 5 inches (11–13 cm), with the tail frequently accounting for two-thirds of this. The hatchlings could easily be mistaken for a different species: They are brown or olive with white spots on their flanks and back, and no sign of the blue eyespots that give the species its name. It takes three years for them to become sexually mature.

⊝ *Until recently the El Hierro giant lizard,* Gallotia simonyi, *was believed to be extinct. It is, in fact, reduced to a small colony surviving only in the remote and inaccessible north of the island of El Hierro. These lizards are now strictly protected.*

The Giant Lizards of the Canary Islands

The Canary Islands belong to Spain even though they are closer to the west coast of Africa. There are seven islands and numerous small offshore islets. They are home to seven species of lacertids, although the distribution is complicated because some islands have more than one species, and some species live on more than one island. The Canary Island lacertids are thought to have originated in North Africa and are most closely related to the sand racers, *Psammodromus* species. They probably reached the eastern islands first and spread westward over millions of years.

These giant lizards all belong to the genus *Gallotia*, which is endemic to the archipelago. Four are of a moderate size, ranging from 4 to 6 inches (10–15 cm) long from snout to vent, but three are very large, with a snout-to-vent length of about 8 to 10.6 inches (20–27 cm). The tail adds another 140 to 170 percent to these lengths. Scientists think that these species may have been much larger in the recent past—perhaps up to 15 inches (40 cm) long from snout to vent and weighing more than 4.4 pounds (2 kg).

Apart from their large size, these lizards also share another characteristic with island reptiles elsewhere: a tendency toward extinction. The El Hierro giant lizard, *G. simonyi*, was presumed extinct in 1940 but was rediscovered in 1999. A population of about 300 remains, restricted to a small part of their once islandwide distribution. It is an herbivorous species with modified teeth and digestive tract. The La Gomera giant lizard, *G. gomerana*, is also a vegetarian and is in a worse predicament. Until it was rediscovered in 1999, it had not been seen since the 1870s. There are no more than 10 individuals living in a small area at the bottom of a rocky cliff. The largest of all species, the Tenerife giant lizard, *G. goliath*, measuring 17.7 inches (45 cm) from snout to vent and with a presumed total length approaching 4 feet (1.2 m), lived on Tenerife, but it has disappeared altogether and is only known from fossils.

The fossil record tells us that all the giant lizards were once abundant. They became rare and extinct in one case when humans settled on the islands. They would have been hunted for food, but the most damaging activities would have been grazing by goats, which destroyed the habitat. Domestic cats also hunt and kill lizards. These pressures may have tipped the balance in favor of the smaller insectivorous species at the cost of the large herbivorous ones. Of the "giant" species only the Gran Canaria giant lizard, *G. stehlini*, is still common, living in humid gorges at densities of up to 1,000 per 2.5 acres (1 ha). There are no small lacertids to compete with them on Gran Canaria.

Common name Viviparous lizard
(European common lizard)

Scientific name *Lacerta vivipara*

Family Lacertidae

Suborder Sauria

Order Squamata

Size 6 in (15 cm) long

Key features Small but robustly built with a cylindrical body, short legs, and a long tail; head short and deep with a rounded snout; neck thick; color and markings highly variable; most are some shade of brown but can also be olive or gray; females often have a plain back with a single dark stripe down the center and dark markings on the flanks; males are darker overall and have small markings consisting of light spots with black edges (ocelli); underside can be white, yellow, or orange

Habits Diurnal; mainly terrestrial

Breeding Most give birth to live young with litters of 3–11 born after a gestation of 8–13 weeks; some populations lay eggs

Diet Small invertebrates; also ants' eggs and larvae

Habitat Very adaptable but absent from forests, cultivated fields, and grazed meadows

Distribution Most of Europe except the Mediterranean region but including northern Spain east to north Asia as far as the Pacific coast and Sakhalin Island, Russia, and Hokkaido Island, Japan

Status Common in suitable habitat

Similar species All small lacertids are difficult to identify in the field, but the common lizard is usually darker than most; the others tend to have slightly flattened body shapes

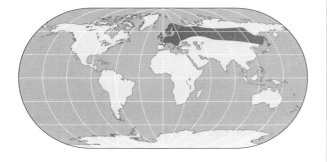

Viviparous Lizard *Lacerta vivipara*

Despite its insignificant appearance, the viviparous lizard is robust and a survivor. It lives farther north than any other reptile and has one of the largest continuous ranges of any lizard.

THE VIVIPAROUS LIZARD OCCURS in Lapland and along the shore of the Barents Sea in Arctic Russia. Its distribution reaches 70°N in Norway—over 200 miles (322 km) inside the Arctic Circle and farther north than any other reptile. Its range is huge—from the Atlantic coast of Ireland and France across Europe and the vast steppes of Central Asia to the Pacific Ocean in China and Russia and even to the islands of Sakhalin (Russia) and Hokkaido (Japan). It has probably the largest continuous range of any lizard and possibly of any nonmigratory vertebrate.

Varied Habitat

Within this range it is very common in parts but scarce or absent in others. It has certain habitat requirements and struggles to live where they are not available. It needs a fairly humid environment and often lives among grass and other lush vegetation that retains moisture. In the north of its range it lives in lowlands and occurs on damp heaths, bogs, dunes, sea cliffs, and road and railway embankments. It needs open spaces to bask in and is most often seen at the edges of paths, clearings, or among piles of logs or rocks. Small colonies quickly disappear if their habitat becomes overgrown to the point where they cannot bask. The lizard also occurs on mountains up to 8,200 feet (2,500 m), where it is restricted to damp meadows, moors, marshes, and ditches.

Despite a long list of potential habitats, it is absent from intensively cultivated land, dense forests, and short turf except at the edges of these habitats, where there is more of a patchwork of vegetation types and open spaces. In the north and in mountains it is most likely to be seen on south-facing banks and

embankments. Railway cuttings have provided it with a corridor into towns and cites, and it can also be found in cemeteries, where it is sometimes seen basking on stonework.

In particularly favorable places to the north of its range with ample basking sites and plenty of food, it can occur in very high densities, sometimes as many as 40 to 400 lizards per acre (100–1,000 per ha). At these densities lizards appear to be everywhere, basking in every available clear space and clambering through vegetation in search of food.

Viviparous lizards are good swimmers and sometimes enter water voluntarily to move from one tussock of grass to another (in flooded marshes, for example) or to catch insects floating on the surface. They will also dive to the bottom to escape from predators and can stay under water for several minutes.

⊕ Viviparous lizards hunt small invertebrates such as insects, spiders, snails, and earthworms. They stun their prey by shaking it before swallowing it whole.

Prey and Predators

Viviparous lizards feed on small invertebrates, especially spiders, caterpillars, flies, and other species. They will also eat ants' eggs and larvae (but not adult ants, apparently). Large prey items are grasped in the mouth and shaken or bashed to death before being swallowed. Caterpillars are sometimes chewed from end to end to extract the insides while the skin is left, but distasteful caterpillars, as well as wasps and bees, are rejected.

The lizards' main natural predators are birds, including kestrels, buzzards, and members of the crow family; small mammals such as weasels and hedgehogs; and reptiles such as larger lizards and adders, *Vipera* species, smooth snakes, *Coronella austriaca*, and whip snakes, *Coluber* species, where they occur. In places viviparous lizards are the staple diet of the adder, *V. berus*. In towns and villages viviparous lizards are hunted by domestic chickens, cats, garden birds, and children. Their main line of defense is to run away and hide in dense vegetation or, if caught, to shed their tail. Urban and suburban populations of viviparous lizards often have a higher incidence of broken and regrown tails than those living in more natural habitats.

Young viviparous lizards, which are very small, are also eaten by spiders, frogs,

toads, slow worms, and a wide range of other opportunistic predators. The number of viviparous lizards that survive to the age of one year may be as low as 10 percent. However, once they reach adult size after two or three years, they have fewer predators and can live for as long as 12 years.

Temperature Regulation

Viviparous lizards are classic "shuttling thermoregulators." In other words, they bask in the sun until they have raised their body temperature to their preferred level, then they go off and do other things. They may hunt for food or search for a mate and return to bask if they need to top up their body temperature. They aim to raise their temperature to about 86°F (30°C), which is optimum for most populations, although those living in mountainous districts regularly operate at temperatures as much as 9°F (5°C) below this.

Obviously, the periods of time between basking sessions will vary according to the ambient temperature, but on days during spring and fall they usually return to their basking spot within two to five minutes. A patient observer can easily watch this activity pattern unfold. During midsummer they may bask off and on for an hour or two in the morning and again in the evening, but they can maintain their preferred body temperature in the middle of the day without exposing themselves.

In midsummer the first lizards emerge from their nighttime retreats at around 6 A.M. and

⊙ *Although it is adaptable in terms of habitat, the viviparous lizard prefers open, damp areas such as marshes, moors, sand dunes, hedgerows, bogs, and ditches.*

⊙ *In the European sand lizard,* Lacerta agilis, *the male's green coloration is most vivid in the breeding season. The female mates with several males, but lays a single clutch of eggs.*

can still be active at 7 P.M. Occasionally a disturbed individual will disappear from one basking spot only to reappear a few feet away. However, these lizards usually return to the same place, and a favored rock or patch of bare sand will be occupied by the same individual throughout the active season.

Lizard Colonies

Viviparous lizards live in loose colonies often centered on a good basking area, such as a south-facing bank with hiding places and somewhere to spend the winter. Their active season begins as early as February in warmer parts of their range, and they have been seen running around while there is still snow on the ground if the weather is warm. Equally, they may be delayed until April or even May in colder regions. Males and juveniles emerge from hibernation before females.

Mating takes place soon after the lizards emerge from hibernation, usually from late March to early June in England, for instance. Unusually among lizards, males are not strongly

territorial. Most males remain in the same small area, however, and mate with all the females living there. Other males move around the edges of the colony; and although fights between them and the territory holder may break out, they are usually successful in obtaining some matings. Females often mate with more than one male.

Mating is not an elaborate or tender affair. The male simply grasps the female in his jaws and attempts to bring their cloacae together by twisting his body under hers. If she is not receptive, she bites back, and the male usually releases her right away.

Pregnant females bask more often and for longer periods than males or nonpregnant females. On cool days they are reluctant to take cover even when closely approached. They flatten their body to increase the area over which they can absorb the sun's heat and are often quite conspicuous.

The young are born in mid- or late summer. The female finds a secluded place to give birth, and they are usually all born during the course of a day, often within an hour. The babies are enclosed in a thin, transparent membrane at first, but struggle free within minutes and go off in search of food. At birth they measure about 1.5 inches (3.8 cm), of which about half consists of the tail.

The young lizards are very dark in color—almost black—with no markings, and they can be mistaken for insects. By the end of the summer when they enter hibernation, they will have grown to about 3 inches (7.6 cm) long. Their tail will be proportionately longer by then, and their coloration will have become lighter. Signs of the adult's markings will have begun to appear. By the end of their second year they

More Than One Father

In lizards and other animals males are often territorial as a means of guarding their mate—by preventing other males from entering the territory where "their" females live, the territorial males have exclusive access to them. Things are not always (or ever) as simple as that, however. Males that move from one territory to another can often "steal" matings before they are driven off by the territory holder. They are sometimes called "sneaky" males, and in some circumstances there will always be a certain proportion of them. Females accept sneaky males because, by producing litters that have more than one father, they stand a better chance of getting at least some vigorous young—they are not putting all their eggs in one basket, so to speak.

Viviparous lizards are not especially territorial, even though most males tend to stay in the same place and will half-heartedly chase off strange "floating" males that come too near. This should mean that females are often mated by more than one male and therefore that litters of young have mixed paternity. Experiments with wild colonies in France have borne this out. By DNA-testing all the young in each litter (by taking a small sample of tissue from the tip of the tail), researchers found that 30 litters out of a total of 44 tested had more than one father. Of these 28 had at least two fathers, and the other two had at least three fathers. The researchers compared the results with others from different localities in France and with semicaptive colonies. They found that, broadly speaking, their results were typical.

Does this mean that male viviparous lizards are making a mistake by not defending their territories more vigorously? Actually, no. In the European sand lizard, *Lacerta agilis*, which is related to the viviparous lizard but is much more territorial, they found that four out of five clutches (80 percent) contained DNA from more than one male. Other experiments with lizards from other families in different parts of the world showed that the incidence of multiple paternity varied from 25 to 82 percent. Compared with these results, viviparous lizards appear to be no worse off than the more territorial species.

will have reached about 4 inches (10 cm) in total. Males will be sexually mature the following spring when they emerge from hibernation. Females take an extra year to reach breeding age.

Egg Laying or Live-Bearing?

The viviparous lizard lives up to its name over nearly all of its range, but in a few places it lays eggs. (Viviparous means giving birth to live young.) Females from populations in the Pyrenees, northern Spain, and parts of Slovenia lay one clutch of between one and 13 eggs that hatch in four to five weeks. The eggs are sometimes laid in communal sites—as many as 60 have been found together in various stages of development. The most likely explanation is that these localities are warmer than the places where the species occurs farther north.

Live-bearing is an adaptation to a cold environment, because by basking, the female can help the embryos develop more quickly. This helps explain why the species is so successful in cooler environments. Live-bearing places an extra burden on females, however, because they have to carry their offspring for

⬆ *A female viviparous lizard gives birth. The young are enclosed in a transparent membrane and are born after a gestation period of about two to three months.*

longer and may make themselves more vulnerable to predation in the process.

Although it is very unusual for a single species to lay eggs in some parts of its range and give birth to live young in others, it is not such a complicated business as it might seem. The viviparous lizard is, in fact, ovoviviparous. This means that instead of laying its eggs, it simply keeps them in its oviduct until they are ready to hatch and then "gives birth" to fully formed young. The eggshell is reduced to a thin, transparent membrane. If the female

⬆ *Males in the genus* Lacerta *often develop bright coloration during the breeding season, as in this male Schreiber's lizard,* L. schreiberi *from Spain.*

The Relatives

The genus *Lacerta* contains 38 species in all, including a number of newly described ones from Turkey and the Middle East. Another three new species, *L. aranica, L. aurelioi,* and *L. bonnali,* are from very small areas in the Pyrenees on the borders of France and Spain; they were formerly considered to be forms of the Iberian rock lizard, *L. monticola,* a colorful montane species from several mountain ranges in the Iberian Peninsula. Other small species are found in the Balkan region.

Another section of the genus includes a series of larger species, measuring from 8 to 16 inches (20–40 cm) and heavily built. They are commonly referred to as "green lizards," even though they also include the European sand lizard, *L. agilis,* which is often light brown or reddish brown in color (the males, however, develop green flanks in the breeding season). The green lizards are found in central and southern Europe, the Middle East, and parts of North Africa. The remaining species, the eyed lizard, *L. lepida,* is by far the largest of the genus, being many times the size of the viviparous lizard.

deposits them early, as she does in some southern locations, she becomes an egg layer.

Other lizards are genuinely viviparous—the developing embryo derives nourishment from its mother through a placenta. American skinks belonging to the genus *Mabuya* have the most highly developed placentas, with female *M. heathi* from Brazil providing 99 percent of their litters' body mass in this way. Scientists think that viviparity (including ovoviviparity) has arisen independently many times—up to 45 times according to some—in lizards.

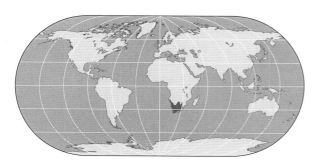

Wedge-snouted sand lizard
(Meroles cuneirostris)

Common names African desert lizards, African sand lizards

Scientific names *Meroles* and *Pedioplanis* sp.

Family Lacertidae

Suborder Sauria

Order Squamata

Number of species *Meroles* 7; *Pedioplanis* 10

Size From 6 in (15 cm) to 8 in (20 cm) long

Key features Slender, long-legged, long-tailed lizards with pointed snouts that are often upturned slightly or wedge shaped; color brown, reddish brown, or buff depending on the surface on which they live, with lines and spots of lighter and darker shades; desert lizards have fringes of hairlike scales beneath their toes, but they are lacking in the sand lizards

Habits Terrestrial and diurnal

Breeding Females lay clutches of up to 8 eggs that hatch after about 60 days

Diet Insects, including beetles, grasshoppers, and locusts; some species eat seeds

Habitat Rocky or sandy deserts

Distribution Southern Africa

Status Very common in suitable habitats

Similar species Sandveld lizards, *Nucras* species

African Desert and Sand Lizards

Meroles and *Pedioplanis*

The arid parts of southern Africa are well endowed with small lacertid lizards. They can be very difficult to distinguish from one another because their markings are often similar.

BETWEEN THEM THE GENERA *Meroles* and *Pedioplanis* contain all the most conspicuous small lacertid lizards of the deserts and semidesert areas in southern Africa. Members of the two genera have slightly different habitat preferences even where their ranges overlap.

Meroles species prefer sandy patches of ground where the fringes beneath their toes help them run across the surface. They occur along the coastal region of southwest Africa, including the Namib Desert, although Knox's desert lizard, *M. knoxii*, occurs farther south in Namaqualand, and the spotted desert lizard, *M. suborbitalis*, occurs farther inland.

By contrast, the *Pedioplanis* species do not have toe fringes and are more at home on rocky or gravely surfaces, often in places where there is scattered vegetation. Some species, such as Burchell's sand lizard, *P. burchelli*, live among rock outcrops. In parts of the Namib Desert, Namaqua sand lizards, *P. namaquensis*, look for insects among the prostrate leaves of ancient *Welwitschia* plants that are dotted over the gravel plains, busily running from plant to plant as they search. These sand lizards are incredibly swift and are active in the heat of the day. When chased, they move across stones and rocks at high speed with sudden and frequent changes of direction, making them difficult to catch. Only rarely do they take cover under shrubs or rocks.

Swimming and Dancing

In the Namib Desert *Meroles* species desert lizards live on the sides of dunes. They are "sand swimmers," diving into loose sand to

↪ *On scorching sand in the Namib Desert the shovel-snouted lizard,* Meroles anchietae, *performs its unusual leg-waving dance.*

↪ *Like other members of its genus, the spotted sand lizard,* Pedioplanis lineocellata, *lacks toe fringes. Its long, slim toes make it very agile over gravel and rocky surfaces.*

escape from predators
and to avoid the worst of the
midday heat. They also spend their nights
below the surface of the sand. These species
have wedge-shaped snouts and countersunk
lower jaws, like the American fringe-toed
lizards, *Uma*, to help them move through the
sand more easily.

The shovel-snouted
lizard, *M. anchietae*,
can tolerate a body
temperature as high as
111°F (44°C). But when
the sand's surface gets
excessively hot, it raises
its tail off the ground
and shuffles its feet in a
comical "dance," lifting
first one front leg and
the opposite back leg,
then changing to the
other two legs.

All these
small lacertids are
insectivorous, feeding on a
wide selection of prey, including
beetles, grasshoppers, and locusts. When
available, they also take large numbers of
termites. The Husab sand lizard, *P. husabensis*
from Namibia, also preys on smaller lizards. The
shovel-snouted lizard, *M. anchietae* (and
possibly other desert lizards), will eat seeds
when insects are in short supply. To find them,
they patrol the bottoms of the leading edges of
dunes, where seeds roll down the slipface and
accumulate. *Pedioplanis* species retreat into
burrows or crevices beneath shrubs or rocks
during the night and during cold weather.

Living and Breeding

Little or nothing is known about the social
structure of the African desert and sand lizards,
but all the species studied so far lay small
clutches of eggs in short burrows or chambers
dug under rocks. The breeding season depends
on local conditions, and some species from
warm places probably breed continuously
throughout the year. The typical clutch size is
from three to six eggs, but the larger species
can lay up to eight at a time. The wedge-
snouted sand lizard, *M. cuneirostris*, however,
usually lays a single egg buried in a tunnel that
it digs in the harder sand between two dunes.

Common name Wall Lizard

Scientific name *Podarcis muralis*

Family Lacertidae

Suborder Sauria

Order Squamata

Size 8.5 in (22 cm) long

Key features Graceful lizard with a narrow head, pointed snout, long tail, and relatively long limbs; coloration extremely variable, and many subspecies are recognized; some forms entirely brown with light and dark markings on their back and sides; in other places they are green (especially males) with extensive black markings; females usually have darker flanks than males and often have a line down the center of the back; markings of males are more likely to be netlike or scattered randomly

Habits Terrestrial and climbing; diurnal

Breeding Female lays clutches of 2–10 eggs that hatch after 6–11 weeks

Diet Insects and spiders

Habitat Dry, open places, including south-facing banks and rock faces, and stone walls around fields and the sides of buildings; often found in villages and the outskirts of larger towns

Distribution Europe from northern Spain and western France through Central Europe and northern Italy to the Peloponnese, Greece; also in Turkey.

Status Very common in suitable habitat

Similar species Many small lacertids from the region are similar and difficult to separate from the wall lizard and each other; locality is often the best means of identification

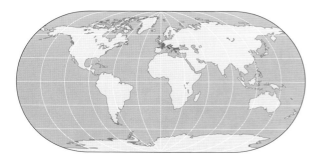

Common Wall Lizard

Podarcis muralis

In many parts of Europe the small lively lizards scurrying about on stone walls and paths, catching insects and pausing to bask occasionally, are most likely to be common wall lizards.

COMMON WALL LIZARDS ARE GENERALISTS and opportunists, and can occur in large numbers—up to 600 per acre (1,500 per ha) in good habitats, often around human dwellings. In some regions wall lizards are hardly ever seen away from houses and are replaced in open countryside by other related but more specialized types of wall lizards. They undoubtedly benefit from the flies and other pests that are attracted to villages and farmyards. They can be seen alternately basking and chasing food, occasionally taking cover in a crevice and slowly moving around during the day to follow the direction of the sun.

Males are territorial but not aggressively so, defending a territory of about 30 square yards (25 sq. m). Females lay from one to three clutches of eggs each year depending on their locality and the abundance of food. A typical clutch consists of about six eggs that are buried, often under a flat stone. They take six to 11 weeks to hatch, and the offspring mature in two to three years.

Lizard Neighbors

In Central Europe the wall lizard has little or no competition. Although it shares the region with the viviparous lizard, *Lacerta vivipara*, the latter prefers moister habitats, and the two are rarely seen side by side. Farther south it overlaps with the ranges of numerous other small lacertids. In Spain and Portugal, for instance, it occurs with the Spanish wall lizard, *Podarcis hispanica*, which is a little more delicately built and is more likely to be seen away from human dwellings on vertical rock faces. Over Italy, Sicily, Sardinia, and Corsica the Italian wall lizard, *P. sicula*,

usually has more bright green on its back, often with a dark line down the center. This species occurs on many Adriatic islands, and there are 48 recognized subspecies! In the Balkan region there are a number of wall lizards, including the Balkan wall lizard, *P. taurica,* and Erhard's wall lizard, *P. erhardii*, but here the common wall lizard is again most likely to be seen around human dwellings.

The wall lizards of the Mediterranean islands are easier to identify because few islands have more than one species—the common wall lizard is absent. In the Balearics, for example, the large islands of Majorca and Minorca are home to Lilford's wall lizard, *P. lilfordi,*

Lacerta or *Podarcis*?

Some small European lacertids are included in the genus *Lacerta,* whereas others are in *Podarcis*. Previously they were all included in *Lacerta,* but changes in their classification in the 1980s and 1990s separated them on the basis of their internal anatomy. In practice, the more delicately built species with a slightly flattened body are *Podarcis* species. Those with a more robust body and deeper head are *Lacerta*, which also includes a number of larger species such as the European sand lizard, *L. agilis*, the eyed lizard, *L. lepida*, and the green lizards (of which *L. viridis* is one). There are no large *Podarcis* species.

⊕ **The coloration of Podarcis muralis varies according to location. There are thought to be about 20 subspecies of this common wall lizard.**

which occurs in a number of color forms, including several melanistic (all-black) populations on offshore islets. Some of these forms, or subspecies, include a large proportion of vegetable material in their diet. The other two Balearic islands are Ibiza and Formentera, and the wall lizard here is *P. pityusensis*, an attractive species that is often bluish in color: One form from the tiny conical islet of Vedra, *P. p. vedrae*, is especially brilliant.

Wall lizard populations on some of the uninhabited islets are unbelievably numerous. The Ibiza wall lizard can reach densities of over 12,000 per acre (30,000 or more per ha), while Lilford's wall lizard easily exceeds this at nearly 18,000 per acre (44,000 per ha) in places. On some islands it is impossible to walk without causing waves of lizards to move away in front of your feet.

Common name Large sand racer

Scientific name *Psammodromus algirus*

Family   Lacertidae

Suborder   Sauria

Order   Squamata

Size   9 in (23 cm) long

Key features Typical lacertid shape with a long tail and limbs and narrow head; scales heavily keeled, overlapping, and ending in a point; tail can be up to 3 times as long as head and body combined, and is stiff; color midbrown with 2 yellowish stripes down the back and another down each flank; males may have blue eyespots at the base of their front legs; hatchlings have reddish flanks

Habits   Terrestrial, climbing occasionally; diurnal

Breeding   Female lays clutches of 2–11 eggs that hatch after 5–6 weeks

Diet   Mainly small insects and spiders

Habitat   Dry, scrubby, or bushy places; often lives around the base of heather, gorse, and other dense bushes; rarely ventures into the open

Distribution Most of Spain and Portugal extending along the Mediterranean coast of France; also North Africa

Status   Common but often overlooked

Similar species The Spanish sand racer, *P. hispanicus*, is smaller and has spots or dashes on its back rather than stripes

Large Sand Racer

Psammodromus algirus

The large sand racer is a handsome lizard that is probably more common than it would appear at first. That is because it has camouflage coloration and a retiring nature.

THE LARGE SAND RACER IS EASILY OVERLOOKED unless it is disturbed while basking, in which case it quickly runs away into the center of a large bush. It favors bushes that are armed with spines or prickles, such as gorse, bramble, or the introduced prickly pear, *Opuntia*, that has spread over much of southern Europe. It occasionally climbs up into bushes to bask or to search for food and also basks on top of logs and in brush piles. It is also found around human dwellings, in gardens, and in overgrown fields. Contrary to its name, it prefers hard-packed soils, such as clay, or stony ground rather than loose sand.

These lizards are very heat tolerant and are active in the middle of the day even in the North African summer. They stay active until dusk. If found in the open, they are often more easily caught than the wall lizards (Lacertidae) since they are slower and less agile. If handled roughly, they squeak and may also do so at other times, for example, when fighting or perhaps as a means of communication.

Their main predators are birds of prey and snakes, and their usual means of defense is to flee and hide in a hole or a crack in the ground. The shape of their scales, with drawn-out, backward-pointing tips, is thought to give the lizards some protection—it would make it hard for snakes, for example, to maneuver them in their mouths to line them up for swallowing.

Unwelcome Visitors

Like many lizards, the large sand racer is often troubled by small red "mites," which are actually mite larvae. In most lizards these pests

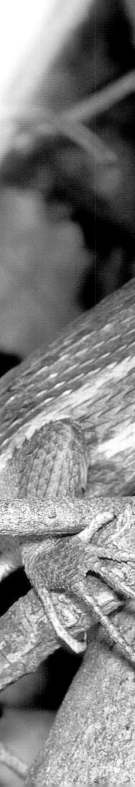

attach themselves to the spaces between the eyes and the surrounding scales or to the area around the eardrum, and cause irritation. They can also cause problems when the lizard tries to shed its skin. Some lizards, including the large sand racer, get around this problem by providing the mite larvae with a special patch of skin with no scales on it, called a "mite pocket," where the mites accumulate.

Breeding

The breeding season starts in about April in most places, and the male follows a female around, attempting to make contact. He bites her neck and twists his body under hers to mate. About 15 to 20 days after mating, the eggs are laid in moist soil in a shallow pit dug by the female. She lays between two and 11 eggs, and may lay a second clutch a few weeks later. The eggs hatch from July onward, and the hatchlings have reddish flanks.

⊖ **Psammodromus algirus** *is the largest member of its genus. It lives in stony, sparsely vegetated areas and can be found sunning itself near human dwellings.*

Other Sand Racers

There are three other members in the genus *Psammodromus*. The Spanish sand racer, *P. hispanicus*, is smaller and lives in Spain and a small part of France. Two species, *P. blanci* and *P. microdactylus*, are similar to each other and occur in North Africa. The latter species is very rare and found only in the Atlas Mountains of Morocco.

The common fringe-toed lizard, *Acanthodactylus erythrurus,* is another lacertid that shares its habitat with the sand racers. It also lives in North Africa and Spain but prefers open ground, including dunes. This species and other members of the genus have a fringe of hairlike scales along the edges of their toes to help them run across loose surfaces. (*Acanthodactylus* means "spiny toes.") On hot surfaces, such as rock or gravel, it often straightens its forelegs when resting to raise the front part of its body clear of the ground and may even lift alternate limbs in turn, in a way similar to that of the shovel-snouted lizard, *Meroles anchietae* from Namibia.

Common name Six-lined grass lizard

Scientific name *Takydromus sexlineatus*

Family   Lacertidae

Suborder   Sauria

Order   Squamata

Size   14 in (36 cm) long, of which up to 80 percent is the tail

Key features Head and body typical of many lacertids but slightly flattened and elongated; however, limbs are short; tail extremely elongated; scales large, keeled, and prominent; keels are aligned and form continuous ridges down the body; basic color brown with white or yellow flanks and a number (not necessarily 6) of light stripes down the back; stripes sometimes green in males, but females are less colorful

Habits   Diurnal and terrestrial; climbs only occasionally

Breeding   Female lays small clutches of eggs, but details are lacking

Diet   Insects and spiders

Habitat   Grassland; found in a variety of places wherever there is a good covering of grasses

Distribution Asia (India, China, Myanmar, Thailand, Indochina, Malaysia, and Indonesia)

Status   Common

Similar species There are 21 other species in the genus, all with similar body plans; *T. sexlineatus*, however, has the largest range and is the most common species over much of the region

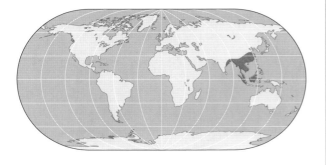

Six-Lined Grass Lizard

Takydromus sexlineatus

The six-lined grass lizard is well adapted to living in grasslands and thick undergrowth. Using its long tail, it "swims" through dense vegetation and can quickly change direction, making it difficult for predators to follow.

LIKE MANY ELONGATED LIZARDS, the six-lined grass lizard does not use its limbs when moving quickly. Instead, it holds them alongside its body to maintain a streamlined body shape. It then moves with a serpentine form of locomotion, waving its head from side to side as it pushes through the undergrowth and using the sides of its body and tail to push against the surface, so that it appears to swim.

Its scientific name, *Takydromus*, means "speed runner." When crawling slowly, however, it brings its legs into play, and they move it forward in a more deliberate, controlled way. In long grass the elongated shape helps the lizard spread its load efficiently, and the tail acts as a counterbalance.

Having a long tail to help with locomotion compromises the lizard's ability to escape by discarding its tail. It gets around this problem by breaking off the minimum length and by rapidly regrowing the tail. That said, the six-lined grass lizard is prepared to use its tail to distract the attention of predators away from its head and body by wiggling the tip. Because it has committed itself to a life in dense vegetation, the lizard's shape makes it less agile on smooth surfaces; if found in the open, it wriggles frantically but makes little progress.

Specialized Niche

The *Takydromus* lizards are the only lacertids to occur widely throughout Asia, although a few species of *Eremias* and *Lacerta* occur in Turkey and neighboring countries and across the Central Asian steppes to China. The grass

lizards seem to have found themselves a niche, because they have radiated into a total of 21 species. They are all similar in shape (with an elongated body, small limbs, and long tail), but they differ in color and markings. Many species are green and difficult to find when they are resting in fresh grass. This is in contrast to the brown species, including *T. sexlineatus*, that are better camouflaged among dead grasses.

Parallels

Lizards in other families, notably the skinks and the alligator lizards, have a shape and means of locomotion similar to those of the six-lined grass lizard, but the closest parallel is the African genus *Chamaesaura*. They are also called grass lizards, although they belong to the Cordylidae, or girdled lizards. There are only three species, and their limbs are reduced by differing amounts. The large-scaled grass lizard, *C. macrolepis*, has no forelimbs at all, and its hind limbs are reduced to vestigial spikes with a single digit. The Cape grass lizard, *C. anguina*, has four limbs, but they are reduced in size and only have one or two digits each. The Transvaal grass lizard, *C. aenura*, has limbs that approach those of the Asian grass lizards in size, and they each have five digits. All these species have heavily keeled scales and are marked with stripes running down their bodies. They are also grass "swimmers," but they use their limbs to keep themselves upright when they stop moving. Like most of their family, they differ from the Asian grass lizards in giving birth to live young.

⊕ *The most obvious distinguishing feature of the six-lined grass lizard is its very long, thin tail, which can be up to four times the length of its body.*

Whiptails and Racerunners

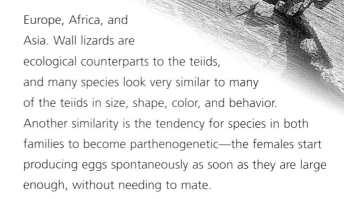

The whiptails, racerunners, and spectacled lizards are sometimes all combined into the Teiidae, with the spectacled lizards forming a subfamily. Here they are separated into two closely related families, the Teiidae and the Gymnophthalmidae. Members of the Teiidae (known as macroteiids if the families are combined) are medium-sized to large lizards from South and Central America. Common names for them include racerunners, whiptails, and tegus. There are 120 species in nine genera.

Teiids range in size from small, slender, streamlined racerunners measuring about 2 inches (5 cm) long from snout to vent in the case of the little striped whiptail, *Cnemidophorus inornatus,* to 24 inches (61 cm) excluding the tail in the tegus, *Tupinambis* species. Their closest relatives (apart from the spectacled lizards) are the members of the Lacertidae, or wall lizards, a family from Europe, Africa, and Asia. Wall lizards are ecological counterparts to the teiids, and many species look very similar to many of the teiids in size, shape, color, and behavior. Another similarity is the tendency for species in both families to become parthenogenetic—the females start producing eggs spontaneously as soon as they are large enough, without needing to mate.

The Species

Most teiids are placed in two genera, *Ameiva* and *Cnemidophorus,* commonly known as the whiptails and the racerunners, and numbering 33 and 60 species respectively. *Ameiva* species are also called jungle racers, while *Cnemidophorus* are variously called whiptails or racerunners. They all have typical lizard shapes with narrow, pointed heads, long limbs, and a long tail. Unlike in the spectacled lizards, limb reduction has not occurred in this family. As their common names suggest, members of both genera are extremely fast moving and alert. The *Ameiva* species are tropical and live in forest clearings and grasslands. They are powerful lizards that are more often heard crashing through undergrowth than seen. Some of them seem to be attracted to human settlements, no doubt due in part to the numbers of insects found there. Members of two smaller genera, *Kentropyx* and *Teius,* are very similar in appearance to *Ameiva.*

Cnemidophorus species are usually striped and can be colored in shades of brown and cream, or in tropical

---

Common name Whiptails, racerunners, and spectacled lizards **Order** Squamata

Family Teiidae 120 species in 9 genera:
Genus *Ameiva*—33 species of jungle racers from Central and South America, including the common jungle racer, *A. ameiva*
Genus *Callopistes*—2 species of false tegus from Chile, Peru, and Ecuador
Genus *Cnemidophorus*—60 species from North, Central, and South America and the West Indies, including the rainbow lizard, *C. lemniscatus,* the six-lined racerunner, *C. sexlineatus,* and the desert grassland whiptail, *C. uniparens*
Genus *Crocodilurus*—1 species from South America, the crocodile tegu, *C. lacertinus*
Genus *Dicrodon*—3 species of desert tegus from Ecuador and Peru
Genus *Dracaena*—2 species of caiman lizards from South America, including the caiman lizard, *D. guianensis*
Genus *Kentropyx*—9 species of whiptails from South America, including *K. pelviceps*
Genus *Teius*—3 species without common names from South America
Genus *Tupinambis*—up to 7 species of tegus from South America, including the Argentine tegu, *T. merianae,* and the black-and-white tegu, *T. teguixin*

Family Gymnophthalmidae 179 species of spectacled lizards in 34 genera, including *Calyptommatus, Bachia, Iphisa, Tretioscincus,* and *Gymnophthalmus*

 SEE ALSO Lizards **44:**8; Wall Lizards **45:**58; Whiptail, Desert Grassland **45:**88; Lizard, Caiman **45:**92; Monitor Lizards **46:**82

① *Larger members of the family Teiidae tend to be carnivores, as in* Callopistes maculatus, *a false tegu from Chile. It is a specialized lizard-feeder.*

Climate and Habitat

Teiids are alert and active during the day. They have a well-defined routine of basking in the morning until their body temperature reaches their preferred level. Then they forage until they need to "top up" their temperature again by basking. Large species may not warm up enough to become active until noon. Whiptails and racerunners prefer higher temperatures than most lizards, and some species do not become active until the temperature reaches 86°F (30°C). For this reason northern species may only be active for six months of the year.

In South and Central America *Ameiva* species usually occur in forest clearings, including areas around villages and farms. This type of habitat gives them plenty of opportunity to bask as well as somewhere to hide at night or if they are threatened. They often bask along the edges of paths and tracks through forests, for instance. If disturbed, they quickly get under cover by running a few yards into the surrounding bushes. There are plenty of egg-laying places for them under rocks or logs. The large tegu lizards, *Tupinambis*, are similar in their habits and often live along the edges of rivers and streams, where sunlight can penetrate. Farther south the Argentine tegus, *T. merianae*, live in stony meadows and along river valleys, often sheltering in burrows that they dig for themselves.

The racerunners in the genus *Cnemidophorus* are more likely to occur in open situations, including scrub and desert in North America and coastal areas in the West Indies and Central America. They are smaller and often venture out into the open on rocky shorelines and sandy beaches. These species begin to bask about two hours after the sun has risen, often in a prominent place such as a rock or a tree stump. By midmorning the temperature will be too hot for them, and they shelter in the shade or in burrows. By midafternoon the heat is less intense, and they reemerge and may stay active until dusk.

Some teiids—notably the caiman lizards, *Dracaena guianensis* and *D. paraguayensis*, and the crocodile tegu, *Crocodilurus lacertinus*—have unusual habitat preferences. All three live in the central Amazon Basin and are semiaquatic. The crocodile tegu has a flattened tail,

regions they may have bright green or blue markings. A high proportion of the *Cnemidophorus* species and some *Kentropyx* species are parthenogenetic. This way of breeding is also found in other lizards (including at least one spectacled lizard, *Gymnophthalmus underwoodi*), but among lizards as a whole it is most common in the racerunners. The desert grassland whiptail, *C. uniparens* from Arizona, is a typical parthenogenetic racerunner.

Of the smaller genera within the family Teiidae there are some specialized lizards. For example, the caiman and crocodile lizards, *Dracaena* and *Crocodilurus*, are semiaquatic, and the tegus, *Tupinambis*, are large lizards that fill the same niche as monitor lizards in Africa, Asia, and Australasia. Three species of *Dicrodon* from Peru and Ecuador are known as desert tegus, and two species of false tegus, *Callopistes flavipunctatus* and *C. maculatus* from Peru and Chile respectively, are attractive lizards that are intermediate between the whiptails and the tegus in size and appearance.

just like a crocodile or alligator, that helps propel it through the water. Its eats frogs, fish, and a variety of invertebrates. The caiman lizards also have a flattened tail, but not to the same extent. They have a double row of raised scales along the back continuing onto the tail. Bony scales on the neck may give some protection against predators. These species also leave the water occasionally and climb trees in search of birds' eggs, although their main diet consists of apple snails, *Ampullaria* species.

Teiids have good eyesight that enables them to spot food at a distance, and their long legs give them the ability to sprint after it. They use the same qualities to see danger and avoid it, so the whiptails are among the hardest lizards to catch. Racerunners and whiptails have been especially successful in colonizing small islands where they are often the dominant species.

Food and Feeding

Whiptails and racerunners are mainly insectivorous, eating a variety of small insects and other invertebrates that come their way. A common tactic is to poke around under dead leaves or wood in the hope of uncovering a meal and simply to grab and swallow it. Members of the whiptail family (Teiidae) are unusual among lizards in having a long, forked tongue like that of a snake, associated with the Jacobson's organ in the roof of the mouth. The only other family that has a similar tongue is the Varanidae, or monitor lizards, which are not closely related. The tegus, *Tupinambis*, are the largest lizards in South America. They eat small mammals, large insects, snails, fish, amphibians, fruit, and carrion. The Chilean false tegu, *Callopistes maculatus*, is a specialized feeder on other lizards, whereas *Dicrodon* are herbivores.

Breeding Activity

All teiids lay soft-shelled eggs, with clutches ranging from three to 30 depending mainly on the size of the species. In the northern and southern parts of the range teiids breed in the spring in response to rising temperatures and longer days. Many of these species hibernate in the winter, and breeding activity takes place soon after they have emerged from hibernation. In more tropical parts of

⊕ *The black-and-white tegu,* Tupinambis teguixin, *comes from South America, where it lives mainly in forest clearings on the ground among leaf litter. It is an agile climber and can also swim quite well.*

the range breeding can go on throughout the year (or most of it)—many of the spectacled lizards probably use this system. Others, however, time their breeding season to coincide with wet or dry seasons.

Conservation

Many islands in the West Indies have introduced a range of predators, especially domestic cats, rats, and dogs, that kill and eat the lizards or their eggs. Goats destroy the

The Spectacled Lizards

The Gymnophthalmidae contains 179 species in 34 genera. They are all small and are sometimes called the microteiids. But because some of them have fused transparent lower eyelids, they are more usually called spectacled lizards. Certain genera are also known as shade lizards, creek lizards, root lizards, and cave lizards, all of which give clues to their lifestyles.

The spectacled lizards and their relatives are secretive species found mostly among leaf litter or under rotting logs in forested parts of South America, although there are a few species in Central America as far north as Mexico and three on West Indian islands. Many species have small limbs: *Calyptommatus* (four species) have lost theirs altogether, while *Bachia* (18 species) have only small flaps that appear to serve no purpose. Their lack of limbs helps them push their way rapidly through leaf litter and dense vegetation.

Evolution has taken exactly the same direction in many species of skinks that live in similar situations. In fact, three genera—*Iphisa, Tretioscincus,* and *Gymnophthalmus*—are very skinklike in appearance and have large glossy scales and cylindrical bodies. *Iphisa elegans* has a very unusual pattern consisting of two rows of enlarged overlapping scales down the center of its back. Other species have their scales arranged in rings around their body.

As far as anyone knows, all the spectacled lizards eat small, soft-bodied invertebrates such as worms, caterpillars, and grubs. Of the species that have been studied, all appear to lay clutches of just one or two small, oval eggs. *Gymnophthalmus underwoodi* (and possibly other species) is parthenogenetic. Apart from this their natural history is poorly known because they are small and easily overlooked, and because they come from parts of the world that are hard to explore. Very few of them have common names.

lizards' habitats by eating the vegetation. A combination of all these problems has led to serious consequences for all native animals, including lizards.

In recent times two species of whiptails, *Ameiva cineracea* and *A. major*, have become extinct from the islands of Guadeloupe and Martinique. *Ameiva polops*, which lives only on the island of St. Croix in the Virgin Islands, is Critically Endangered (IUCN); in addition the St. Lucia racerunner, *Cnemidophorus vanzoi*, is classed as Endangered (IUCN).

The golden spectacled lizard, **Gymnophthalmus speciosus,** *is a representative member of the family Gymnophthalmidae. Its cylindrical body and glossy scales are similar to those of the skinks.*

Common name Jungle racer (common ameiva)

Scientific name *Ameiva ameiva*

Family Teiidae

Suborder Sauria

Order Squamata

Size From 16 in (41 cm) to 24 in (60 cm)

Key features Body stocky; head deep, pointed, and angular and covered in large scales; limbs long; claws also long, especially on hind legs; tail cylindrical and accounts for just over half the total length if it is complete; body scales small and granular; color mainly brown with some areas of green on the back; a pattern of light and dark spots appears on the flanks, often arranged into vague cross-bands

Habits Terrestrial and diurnal

Breeding Female lays clutches of 2–9 eggs; further detail unknown

Diet Insects and small vertebrates, including other lizards

Habitat In clearings and on paths and roadsides in otherwise forested areas

Distribution Northern South America from Panama throughout the Amazon Basin to northern Argentina

Status Common

Similar species There are over 30 other *Ameiva* species and 9 *Kentropyx* species, all of which look quite similar; the jungle racer is larger than most, is the most widespread, and the one most likely to be seen

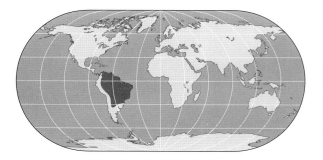

Jungle Racer

Ameiva ameiva

The jungle racer is very conspicuous over much of South America. It is found in tropical open forests, woodlands, and agricultural areas, where it is often the most common species.

A COMMON SIGHT IN SOUTH AMERICA, the jungle racer frequently basks on paths and at the sides of roads, and scuttles away into the safety of bushes and debris if it is disturbed. Many jungle racers go unnoticed, however, since they usually remain stationary and rely on their coloration to protect them. It is only when they think they have been discovered that they crash away through the vegetation. Even so, they soon return to a favored spot once the coast is clear, occupying small patches of sunlight surrounded by plenty of cover.

Sun Lovers

Jungle racers are only active when the temperature reaches 79°F (26°C). At other times they remain hidden under rocks or logs. They are sometimes out on rainy days, however, if it is warm enough. Their preferred body temperature is between 99 and 104°F (37–40°C), and by basking, they can raise it significantly higher than the air temperature. Using measurements taken from a large number of lizards, researchers found that they typically had temperatures that were about 7 to 21°F (4–12°C) above the air temperature, with an average increase of 12 to 14°F (7–8°C).

They are very alert lizards, frequently turning their head to one side and looking over their back to make sure that they are not surprised. Their main

 Closeup of a juvenile jungle racer on a branch in Guiana, showing the patches of bright-green color present on the back and head.

predators are probably fast-moving snakes such as the parrot snakes, *Leptophis* species, birds of prey, and domestic cats.

Egg Layers

In Amazonian Ecuador they breed for about six months of the year, with eggs being laid from July to December. The juveniles hatch out of the eggs from October to April. Over other parts of their range they may breed throughout the year with a small pause during the dry season. The female can lay between two and nine eggs, but a typical clutch consists of four to six eggs. She lays them in a hole in the soil that she excavates herself, often under a log or stump. Lizards living near rivers may use exposed sandbanks as nesting sites.

The Human Factor

It seems that the jungle racer is one of a small number of lizards that benefit from human activities. Its range appears to be increasing as areas of forest are cleared, and it extends its range by spreading along paths, roads, and across fields and plantations. For example, the first record of the species for Costa Rica was made quite recently in a banana plantation in the south of the country. Clearance of forest increases the number of basking places for this sun-loving species, and it also benefits from increased numbers of flies, crickets, and cockroaches that result from such development.

In one site in Ecuador where land was cleared for mineral extraction, jungle racers were not seen at all at the beginning of the project, even though they lived along the edges of a river about 2 miles (3.2 km) away. Once a connecting road was built from the river to the site, they began appearing around the settlement and eventually became one of the most common species. While the jungle racers were spreading, other species were becoming more scarce. The related and similar *Kentropyx pelviceps* favors untouched rain forest; as the habitat of the jungle racer was increasing, that of *K. pelviceps* was being reduced. For a time the two species can live side by side, since the habitat is just about tolerable for both, but the jungle racer will inevitably take over.

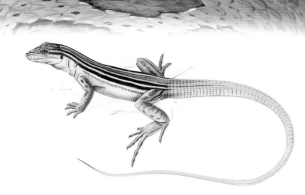

Common name Desert grassland whiptail

Scientific name *Cnemidophorus uniparens*

Family Teiidae

Suborder Sauria

Order Squamata

Size 9 in (23 cm) long

Key features A small, graceful lizard with a long
cylindrical body; long tail accounts for about
two-thirds of total length if complete; head
narrow and pointed; limbs long, especially
the back ones, which also have long toes;
color rich brown with 6 unbroken cream
stripes from the back of the head to the base
of the tail; juveniles have blue tails

Habits Terrestrial and diurnal

Breeding Parthenogenetic; females lay 1–4 eggs
without the help of males; eggs hatch into
more females in 50–55 days

Diet Insects and spiders

Habitat Dry scrub and grassland; open forests in
mountain foothills

Distribution North America (southeastern Arizona,
southwestern New Mexico, and adjacent
parts of Mexico to the south)

Status Common

Similar species Other whiptails, of which there are a
number in the region

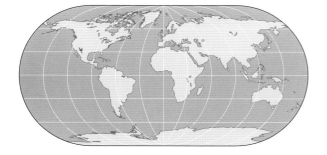

Desert Grassland Whiptail

*Cnemidophorus
uniparens*

*The desert grassland whiptail is a fast-moving,
sun-loving lizard with a terrific capacity for
speed and an interesting life history.*

THE DESERT GRASSLAND WHIPTAIL lives in arid parts of
the American Southwest, rarely emerging until
temperatures reach 86°F (30°C) or more and
basking on the most exposed patches of sand
or rock. Where it extends up into the desert
foothills, it also lives between evergreen oak
trees, sometimes basking on their bases or on
the boulders surrounding them.

Like other whiptails, this lizard is a fast
mover; similar species have been clocked at
15 mph (25 km/h), which is the speed achieved
during a four-minute mile! What's more, it can
keep up this speed for a considerable time. If it
is trying to run down a meal or escape from a
predator, it can race across open ground
without a pause and change direction in the
blink of an eye. It rarely resorts to cover and
prefers to stay in the open and outrun its
enemies. This is a challenging species to catch!

On the other hand, it is sometimes hunted
successfully by whip snakes, such as the
Sonoran whip snake, *Masticophis bilineatus*,
and the coachwhip, *M. flagellum*. Nocturnal
lizard-eating snakes, such as lyre snakes,
Trimorphodon biscutatus, long-nosed snakes,
Rhinocheilus lecontei, and spotted night snakes,
Hypsiglena torquata, are plentiful in the region
where it lives, and they are probably its most
effective predators. Their strategy is to nose
around in crevices and burrows at night, hoping
to catch diurnal lizards while they are sleeping.

Single Parents

The aspect of its natural history that separates
the desert grassland whiptail from most other
lizards is its reproductive biology. The clue is in
its scientific name—*uniparens* means "one

Parthenogenesis—How Widespread Is It?

Although many invertebrates are parthenogenetic (aphids and water fleas, for example), there are only a few fish, a few amphibians, one snake, and about 30 species of lizards that reproduce in this way (that we know of). Since not all the species are closely related to each other, parthenogenesis has evidently evolved independently among lizards several times.

Parthenogenetic species are found among the Agamidae (the butterfly agamas, *Leiolepis* species); the Chamaeleonidae (a dwarf chameleon, *Brookesia affinis*); several geckos (including *Hemidactylus garnotii* and *Lepidodactylus lugubris*); the Gymnophthalmidae (Underwood's spectacled lizard, *Gymnophthalmus underwoodi*); the Teiidae (several whiptail lizards and also *Kentropyx suquiensis* from Argentina); and the Xantusiidae (the yellow-spotted night lizard, *Lepidophyma flavimaculatus*). It is also possible that a member of the Iguanidae, one of the chuckwallalike *Phymaturus* species from southern Chile and Argentina, reproduces by parthenogenesis.

parent." This is an all-female species that can reproduce without having mated. There are no males, and all individuals are female clones. Occasionally females will behave like males and go through a false courtship and copulation sequence. In whiptail lizards this behavior increases the clutch size of the female, but in some other parthenogenetic species it has the opposite effect (in other words, it lowers the reproductive output). The reasons for this anomaly are not understood.

Parthenogenesis in lizards was first discovered in 1958 by the Russian herpetologist Ilya Darevsky. The first species known to be parthenogenetic was a lacertid, *Lacerta saxicola*, since renamed (fittingly) *Darevskia saxicola*. Following this, other parthenogenetic species were discovered, including several more lacertids from the Caucasian region, often after workers realized that all museum specimens were females. It later turned out that

⊕ *Although it has many predators, few can outrun the desert grassland whiptail. Because it is so fast and agile, it is able to spend much of its time in the open.*

parthenogenesis is especially common among whiptail lizards, and the species most thoroughly investigated is the desert whiptail lizard. Confirmation came with an experiment in which skin grafts were made on desert grassland whiptail lizards from widely separated parts of their range. They all accepted small patches of skin from each other, as you would expect if they were all clones. Grafts made between individuals of a sexually reproducing species, the western whiptail lizard, *C. tigris*, were invariably rejected.

How Parthenogenesis Works

There are several ways in which all-female species reproduce. The European pool frogs, *Rana* species, reproduce by a method called hybridogenesis, and some North American mole salamanders, *Ambystoma* species, use a method called gynogenesis. Both systems require a male to initiate cell division, even though his genetic material is not incorporated into the resultant eggs. The desert whiptail lizard follows a third system, parthenogenesis, in which males are not required at all.

The desert grassland whiptail is the result of hybridization and back-crossing between the little striped whiptail, *C. inornatus*, and the Texas spotted whiptail, *C. gularis*. In normal sex cells each chromosome divides once, and each resulting strand becomes part of a gamete (that is, sperm or ovum) that then combines with the equivalent chromosome from the opposite sex in a process known as meiosis. In the desert grassland whiptail, however, division of the sex cells is abnormal—the cells undergo a

⊕ **The rainbow lizard, Cnemidophorus deppei** *from Costa Rica, has beautiful bright markings. Like the desert grassland whiptail, it is very fast and agile.*

⊖ *The coastal whiptail,* **Cnemidophorus tigris multiscutatus** *from Baja California, Mexico, has a checkered appearance. It is closely related to the desert grassland whiptail.*

preliminary doubling of the chromosomes before meiosis, resulting in cells with four strands of each chromosome (4N). They divide to give 2N (diploid) instead of the normal 1N (haploid) pattern, and the ova develop into offspring that are genetically identical to the mother. They do not need the complementary chromosomes that would normally be provided by the male. All the young produced are also females and can lay eggs without mating.

Parthenogenesis—Pros and Cons

A parthenogenetic breeding system has advantages and disadvantages. On the plus side, species can reproduce without males and are therefore more likely to colonize fresh territory—it only takes a single female (even a juvenile or an egg) to move in. This is especially helpful to species such as some geckos that often raft to new islands.

Another advantage, and one that applies to the desert grassland whiptail, is the very fast rate at which populations can increase. In a population with the usual 50:50 sex ratio only half produce eggs or young, whereas in parthenogenetic species they all produce offspring. Since population growth is exponential, there is a dramatic increase after just a few generations. Assuming that every female lays 10 eggs a year, the population is 10 at the end of the first year. Each of those females will produce 10 eggs the following year, making 100. By the end of the third year there will be 1,000, and so on.

In contrast, in a sexually breeding species there will be five females at the end of the first year. They will produce a total of 50 by the end of the second year, but about half will be males. The 25 females will produce a total of 250 young the third year, but again, only half will be females. Leaving predation and other dangers aside, the reproductive population of the parthenogenetic species after just three years will already be eight times that of the normal species (1,000 versus 125).

But if parthenogenetic species are so successful, why aren't there more of them? Parthenogenetic individuals are all clones. They are genetically identical to each other; unlike in sexually reproducing species, there is no variability. Because the adaptation of a species is based on natural selection, where those most suited to the environment survive and the others do not, variability becomes important if the environment changes—at least some will be able to survive. Because parthenogenetic species consist of identical clones, if the conditions change drastically even over a long period, they will probably all die off.

There are two conclusions to be drawn. First, many parthenogenetic species are probably quite "young." They arose only a few hundred years ago, have thrived until now, but may not survive very much longer. Others will take their place if conditions change. The other scenario is that they will act like "weeds," moving from place to place to track patches of suitable habitat. They are quick to exploit new opportunities, increase quickly, and then move on.

Common name Caiman lizard

Scientific name *Dracaena guianensis*

Family Teiidae

Suborder Sauria

Order Squamata

Size From 36 in (91 cm) to 42 in (107 cm) long

Key features A very distinctive lizard; body stocky; head large; large studlike scales present on the neck; numerous raised keels on the back are arranged into rough lines; keels on the tail form a pair of saw-tooth crests; body color bright green, olive, or brown; head orange

Habits Semiaquatic; diurnal

Breeding Female lays clutches consisting of 2 eggs

Diet Mostly aquatic snails

Habitat Amazonian forest in swamps, along riversides, and in flooded areas

Distribution South America (Amazon Basin)

Status Rarely seen, probably because its preferred habitat is difficult to explore

Similar species There is another caiman lizard farther south, *D. paraguayensis*

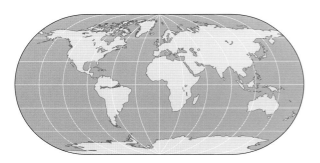

Caiman Lizard

Dracaena guianensis

A strange but spectacular teiid that looks more like a small crocodilian than a lizard, the caiman lizard is one of three members of its family that lead a semiaquatic lifestyle.

CAIMAN LIZARDS SPEND MOST OF THEIR TIME in the water in flooded forests, swamps, and streams bordering the Amazon River. They frequently climb into trees and bushes to bask on the branches that hang out over the water. They are good swimmers, usually swimming near the surface with their head out of the water. The two rows of raised keels on their back and tail give them extra thrust through the water, just as they do with their namesake, the caiman.

Snail-Eaters

When hunting, the lizards enter deep water and walk across the bottom, flicking their forked tongue in and out as they nose around under waterlogged debris such as leaves and branches. Their most important source of food is apple snails, *Ampullaria* species. Once they find a snail, they pick it up in their mouth and bring their head up out of the water, tilting the snout up so that the snail rolls toward the back of their jaws, where the teeth are flattened and molarlike. Once it is there, the lizard uses the full force of its jaws like a pair of nutcrackers. Having crushed the substantial shell, the lizard manipulates it in its mouth until it can swallow the soft part of the animal and discard the shell fragments with its tongue. During the dry season, when snails are not available, the lizard may switch its diet and climb into trees in search of insects and possibly even birds' eggs.

Lifestyle

Almost nothing is known about the caiman lizard's behavior in the wild. The male has a gigantic head that appears out of proportion to the rest of its body, and he apparently uses it to demonstrate his dominance. Having found a

→ *Caiman lizards have very large heads, powerful jaws, and strong teeth that enable them to crush the shells of snails, which are their main prey items.*

→ *Dracaena paraguayensis occurs farther south than the caiman lizard. Both species are graceful swimmers, folding their legs back against the body and swimming in a serpentine manner with the head just above water.*

on branches overhanging the water, into which it escapes if necessary, and it feeds on earthworms, tadpoles, frogs, and fish. Like the caiman lizards, the male's head is larger than the female's and is reddish in color, whereas the female's head is brown. The similarity with caiman lizards ends there, however, since the Chinese crocodile lizard gives birth to live young. Because their names are similar, it is important not to confuse the Chinese crocodile lizard with the South American crocodile tegu, *Crocodilurus lacertinus*, which belongs to the same family as the caiman lizard.

female, he follows her around to guard her from the advances of other males. Females have been found with two eggs in their oviducts, but nobody knows where they lay them or how long they take to hatch. Juveniles are more colorful than adults. Both adults and juveniles retreat into holes in the riverbanks if they feel under threat.

Parallels

Superficially, the lizard most similar to the caiman lizards is the Chinese crocodile lizard, *Shinisaurus crocodilurus*. This semiaquatic species is a member of the small family Xenosauridae and lives in slow-moving streams in a small area of southern China. It basks

The Other Caiman Lizard

The only other member of the genus is the Paraguayan caiman lizard, *Dracaena paraguayensis*. It is brown or olive in color with lighter markings loosely arranged into transverse stripes. Even less is known about this species than the Amazonian caiman lizard. As well as in Paraguay, it lives in the Mato Grosso region of Brazil and in part of lowland Bolivia. This region is within the immense wetland complex known as the Pantanal. It is one of the world's richest ecosystems, covering nearly 80,000 square miles (207,200 sq. km) during the rainy season, when rivers overflow and flood the surrounding forest.

Local people think the Paraguayan caiman lizard is venomous. They believe that when it grows up, it sheds its legs and turns into a snake. This may stem from the fact that when the lizard drops its tail, the tail continues to wriggle and can resemble a small viper.

Common name Tegu (black-and-white tegu)

Scientific name *Tupinambis teguixin*

Family   Teiidae

Suborder   Sauria

Order   Squamata

Size   To 43 in (109 cm), of which just under half is the tail

Key features Large and powerful lizard with a cylindrical body; tail thick; head long; snout narrow; limbs are also powerful and end in long claws; the whole lizard is covered with small shiny scales that give it a glossy appearance; adults boldly marked in black and white or black and yellow, but juveniles are bright green

Habits   Terrestrial and diurnal

Breeding   Female lays 7–30 eggs that hatch after about 12 weeks

Diet   Insects, spiders, other lizards, birds and their eggs, small mammals; also eats carrion

Habitat   Rain forests in clearings and along river courses

Distribution South America (Brazil, Peru, Colombia, Venezuela, Ecuador, northern Argentina, Uruguay, Bolivia, Guiana, Surinam, French Guiana); Trinidad

Status   Common in suitable habitat, although never in large numbers

Similar species Up to 6 other species in the genus occur throughout South America, all differing slightly in coloration, but the validity of some is in doubt; otherwise there are no similar species; juveniles could possibly be mistaken for jungle racers, *Ameiva* species

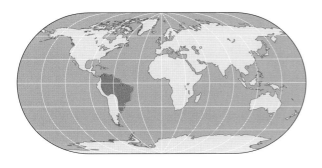

Tegu

Tupinambis teguixin

The tegu is among the world's largest lizards. In many of the places where it lives it fills the same ecological niche as small mammalian predators.

TEGUS ARE VERY POWERFUL LIZARDS and are able to catch large insects, other lizards, snakes, nestling birds, and small mammals. They are particularly fond of birds' eggs, and they often raid nests, including those of domestic fowl. A related species, the Argentine tegu, *Tupinambis merianae*, also eats fruit and has even been known to beg food from picnickers in public parks. The common tegu, however, is a confirmed carnivore.

Adult *T. teguixin* have quite well-defined home ranges centered on their burrows, where they can hunt most successfully without competition from neighbouring tegus. They use their long, sensitive tongue to detect potential prey by picking up scent particles from the atmosphere. Then they scratch or dig at the surface using their powerful limbs.

When they find a prey item, they grasp it in their jaws and, if it is large, bash it repeatedly against the ground in order to stun it. Once it stops struggling, they normally bolt it down in one piece, although they may tear large items into smaller pieces. Full-grown tegus feed mainly in the afternoon after they have raised their body temperature to about 86°F (30°C), but juveniles forage throughout the day.

Forest Dwellers

The natural habitat of tegus is dense primary rain forest. They are often found near the edges of wide rivers and lakes or in forest clearings, where they can use the open spaces to bask. They live in burrows that they either dig for themselves or take over from small mammals.

Tegus swim well; if their habitat becomes temporarily flooded, they make their way to

Lizard Parallels

The American tegus are the ecological counterparts of the monitor lizards, which are found only in Africa, Asia, and Australasia. Apart from having glossy scales, tegus could easily be mistaken for monitors—they have a raised, ambling gait, powerful limbs, a long and constantly flickering tongue, and natural curiosity. Like tegus, monitors often live in areas where there are few other predators and have been quick to fill this niche. And like the tegus, some monitor lizards associate humans with food and are especially common around villages and popular picnic sites. Finally, a number of monitor lizards also make use of termite nests to lay their eggs, taking advantage of the constant temperature and the security provided by the efforts of the insects.

higher ground to wait until the water level subsides. In addition, tegus often make their homes on the outskirts of villages and towns, where human activities create artificial clearings. They are also attracted by the prospect of finding easy prey and may even become pests by raiding poultry farms to steal the eggs. If they are unfortunate enough to get caught, they provide a welcome addition to the diet of local people.

Courtship and Egg Laying

The tegus breed at the start of the dry season so that their eggs are ready to hatch during the wet season, when there is plenty of food around. Courtship in tegus is dramatic. The male approaches the female sideways, puffing himself up and standing up on stiff legs to make himself look bigger. He makes regular snorting or "sneezing" sounds. Then he approaches her, grabs her neck in his jaws, and holds her body down with his hind legs. He twists his body under hers so that their cloacae are next to each other. Copulation can then take place.

When the female is ready to lay her eggs, she may dig a burrow in the soil or in leaf litter in a forest clearing; but she often chooses a termite mound. She breaks into the base of the mound using her powerful legs and claws, and makes a nest chamber.

⊖ All tegus are black with yellow or white bands across the back. The small glossy scales are arranged in regular rings around the body. This is Tupinambis teguixin in Trinidad.

She lays up to 30 eggs there, and the termites quickly repair the damage and seal in the eggs. The temperature and humidity in the mound are carefully controlled by the termites, so it makes an ideal incubator. The eggs hatch after about three months, and the young break out of the termite mound after it has been softened by rain. In contrast to the adults, they are bright green with black spots.

Warming Up

Like all reptiles, tegus rely on the sun to maintain a suitable body temperature, ideally about 86°F (30°C) in their case. They are not active at temperatures much below this. They raise their body temperature by occasional basking throughout the day. Large individuals take a long time to warm up and therefore do not emerge from their burrows until the middle of the day; they remain sluggish when the weather is cool.

In the colder parts of their range the tegus sometimes remain hiding in their burrows for several weeks during the worst of the cold weather, although they do not hibernate in the same way as the species from farther south.

Tegus' enemies include birds of prey, cats, and snakes. Juveniles are more vulnerable than adults, which have relatively few enemies by the time they reach full size. They defend themselves by using their tail as a whip or by biting and clawing their way out of trouble. In extreme situations they may discard their tail; although they can grow a new one, it is never quite as long as the original.

Hunting and the Skin Trade

Since tegus can have a habit of raiding poultry farms to steal the eggs, it is not surprising that they are often considered to be vermin. Over much of South America tegus are hunted and trapped by local people. Apparently they make good eating, and their skins are valuable for fashion goods. Lizard skin is a significant source of income for villagers, and the number of tegus captured for that purpose is estimated to be between one and three million each year.

Populations living near towns and villages are the most vulnerable, while those in remote, forested areas are fairly safe—at least for the time being.

The Argentine tegu, *T. merianae*, however, lives only in the eastern part of Argentina. It inhabits open land often covered by tall clumps of pampas grass and is rarer than *T. teguixin*.

⊖ *Tegus are capable of eating large prey, which they can stun by beating it against the ground. Here* **T. teguixin** *is tackling a rattlesnake,* **Crotalus durissus.**

Tegu Names and Species

The name "tegu" comes from an Amazonian Indian word that simply means lizard. Names within the genus *Tupinambis* are confusing. *Tupinambis teguixin* was previously used for the Argentine tegu, which is now called *T. merianae*. The black-and-white tegu discussed here used to be called *T. nigropunctatus*, a name that is no longer valid. Much information that was gathered in the past about these lizards is no longer useful because there is no way of knowing which species it related to.

The Argentine tegu is a hardy species that hibernates during the cold southern winter. It grows slightly larger than the black-and-white tegu. Most tegus in the pet trade are black-and-white tegus and are recognizable by their color and their small, shiny scales, which are similar to those of skinks. They are nervous and hard to tame. The Argentine tegu is rare in captivity, although it is bred in small numbers. It can be distinguished by small beadlike scales like those of a Gila monster.

Tupinambis duseni is a Brazilian species whose range overlaps that of *T. teguixin*. It is reddish in color, but its validity as a species is uncertain. A similar situation exists with *T. longilineus* (also from Brazil). *Tupinambis palustris*, which translates as "marsh tegu," was only described in 2002 from Rondonia, Brazil. It differs from *T. teguixin* in slight details of markings. *Tupinambis quadrilineatus* from central Brazil is also a recent addition to the genus, described in 1997. The seventh species is the red tegu, *T. rufescens*, which is restricted to Argentina and is a heavy-bodied species with reddish-brown coloration. Like the other Argentine species, *T. merianae*, it hibernates during the cooler months of the year.

Girdle-Tailed and Plated Lizards

The girdle-tailed and plated lizards are sometimes combined in a single family (Cordylidae) with two subfamilies, the Gerrhosaurinae and the Cordylinae. However, it is more usual to treat them as two separate families. Both families are African, but the plated lizards have a slightly wider distribution overall than the girdle-tailed lizards.

The Cordylidae

There are 55 species of girdle-tailed, or girdled lizards, in four genera. The Cordylidae is the only family that is restricted to the continent of Africa (the plated lizards also live on Madagascar). Its members typically have a

flattened body that is rectangular or box shaped in cross-section with a fold along the sides. They have large scales arranged in regular rows across the body and whorls of large spiny scales on the tail. Despite the anatomical similarities that link them all in the same family, the four genera are very distinctive and easily separated, even superficially.

The grass lizards, *Chamaesaura*, are elongated species with long tails and reduced limbs. There are three species, and they all give birth to between five and 12 live young. They live in grass and thick vegetation, and move through it by swimming movements. Although they will shed their tail if necessary, only the minimum is broken off. Without a tail they are severely handicapped and can move only slowly and noisily. Fortunately, the lost portion is quickly regrown. Their brown color provides good camouflage among dry vegetation.

The 30 species of girdled lizards, *Cordylus*, have stocky bodies. Their triangular heads are covered with large scales, and the scales around their bodies are in rings, or "girdles." They are among the most characteristic lizards of southern Africa, where there is hardly a rock outcrop without a colony of one species or another. Several species have very small ranges because the rock formations on which they live are isolated from each other by large tracts of unsuitable habitat; several species have only been recognized as distinct in recent years. The genus has its stronghold in South Africa, but these lizards occur up into East Africa. One species, *C. rivae*, has most of its range inside Ethiopia.

Cordylus species bask in the most exposed places, for example, on sheer rock faces or on top of boulders, and

---

Common name Girdle-tailed and plated lizards **Order** Squamata

Family Cordylidae 55 species of girdle-tailed lizards in 4 genera:
Genus *Chamaesaura*—3 species of grass lizards from South Africa, including the Cape grass lizard, *C. anguina*
Genus *Cordylus*—30 species of girdle-tailed lizards from southern Africa, including the armadillo lizard, *C. cataphractus*, the Cape girdle-tailed lizard, *C. cordylus*, the sungazer, *C. giganteus*, and the black girdle-tailed lizard, *C. niger*
Genus *Platysaurus*—15 species of flat lizards from southern Africa, including Broadley's flat lizard, *P. broadleyi*, and the common flat lizard, *P. intermedius*
Genus *Pseudocordylus*—7 species of crag lizards from southern Africa, including the graceful crag lizard, *P. capensis,* and the Cape crag lizard, *P. microlepidotus*

Family Gerrhosauridae 32 species of plated lizards in 6 genera:
Genus *Angolosaurus*—1 species from Namibia and southern Angola, the desert plated lizard, *A. skoogi*
Genus *Cordylosaurus*—1 species of dwarf plated lizards from southern Africa, *C. subtessellatus*
Genus *Gerrhosaurus*—6 species from southern and East Africa, including the giant plated lizard, *G. validus*
Genus *Tetradactylus*—6 species of seps lizards from southern Africa as far north as Tanzania, including the common seps, *T. tetradactylus*
Genus *Tracheloptychus*—2 species from Madagascar with no common names
Genus *Zonosaurus*—16 species of plated lizards from Madagascar, including the common plated lizard, *Z. madagascariensis,* and the western plated lizard, *Z. laticaudatus*

 SEE ALSO Lizard, Black Girdle-Tailed **45**:102; Lizard, Armadillo **45**:104; Beaded Lizards **46**:74; Monitor, Borneo Earless **46**:100

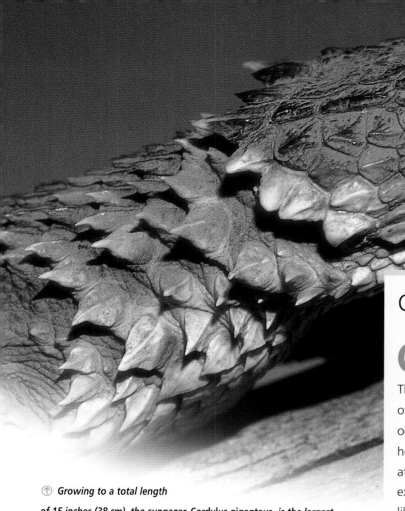

⬆ **Growing to a total length**

of 15 inches (38 cm), the sungazer, Cordylus giganteus, **is the largest member of its genus. It raises the front part of its body to catch the sun.**

can easily be seen from a distance. But they run quickly to cover if approached. The largest species, the sungazer, *C. giganteus*, is an exception. It lives in grasslands and digs burrows up to 6 feet (1.8 m) long. They are mostly north-facing to catch the sun. Each burrow is occupied by a single adult, although they will often share their burrow with one or more juveniles. During the day they bask at the entrance to the burrow or on a nearby termite mound facing the sun. They hibernate in their burrows in the winter, during which time small frogs sometimes live there with them. All the girdled lizards are live-bearers.

The 15 species of flat lizards, *Platysaurus*, are well named because they are extremely flattened, and their bodies are covered with small granular scales. Males are brilliantly colored and very territorial, whereas the females are mostly brown with stripes. Their shape allows them to enter very narrow cracks in rocks or under rock flakes from which it is almost impossible to extract them. Different species favor different rock types, such as

Osteoderms

Osteoderms are bony plates underlying the scales of certain reptiles, including crocodilians, turtles, and some lizards. They are embedded in the inner layer of skin (dermis) and consist of a spongy outer layer and a compact inner layer. They usually occur on the animal's back and sides, and sometimes on its head, as in the beaded lizards (Helodermatidae). They are loosely attached to each other in rows, allowing the skin to flex and expand, but at the same time providing a layer of bony armor, like chain mail. Even so, species with osteoderms tend to be more rigid than those without. In tortoises and turtles the osteoderms fused with the vertebrae to form the protective carapace (shell) and with the sternum to form the plastron (underside of the shell).

Osteoderms occur in all plated lizards and in the girdle-tailed lizards, *Cordylus*, but are absent in other members of the Cordylidae. Elsewhere among the lizards osteoderms occur in the Anguidae (alligator and glass lizards), the skinks, and the Borneo earless monitor, *Lanthanotus borneensis*, among others.

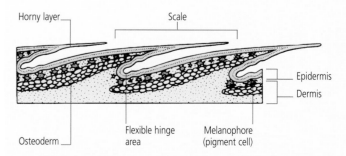

Cross-sectional diagram of the skin of a slow worm (Anguidae). Like many other lizards, it is heavily armored. Its scales are mostly nonoverlapping with osteoderms.

sandstone or granite, and their distribution coincides with the occurrence of each particular type of rock. This has led to a number of isolated populations that have subsequently evolved further into different species, especially in Zimbabwe. Flat lizards are the only egg-laying species in the family.

The crag lizards, *Pseudocordylus*, are similar to the girdled lizards. However, the scales on their backs, although arranged in rows, are smaller, and the scales on their tails are not as spiky. The six species are all rock dwellers and live in rock crevices usually on hillsides. They have powerful jaws that they use for crushing their prey, which consists mainly of beetles, crickets, and other lizards. The scales on top of the head are thickened with osteoderms to keep the skull from being damaged. Males of several species are brightly colored with orange or yellow flanks. Crag lizards are live-bearers.

The Gerrhosauridae

Plated lizards occur in a variety of habitats in southern Africa and Madagascar. There are 32 species in six genera. They are closely related to the girdle-tailed lizards, but they are all egg layers. They are diurnal, and all of them have rectangular scales with osteoderms. Generally speaking, they are more likely than the girdle-tailed lizards and their relatives to occur in flat, open countryside. Many plated lizards bask in a characteristic posture with their bodies touching the ground and their limbs raised. From this position they sometimes lower their limbs temporarily to push themselves forward an inch or two, still with their underside in contact with the ground.

The dwarf plated lizard, *Cordylosaurus subtessellatus*, is in a genus of its own. It is a small but beautiful species with a chocolate-brown and cream striped body and a long, bright blue tail that is easily broken. It lives among rock outcrops along the southwestern coastal belt of Africa from the Namib Desert through Namaqualand to the Western Cape region. It is quick and agile, and darts back under rock flakes if it is approached too closely, but soon emerges to bask again. From a distance it resembles some of the blue-tailed skinks, such as the five-lined skink, *Eumeces fasciatus*. The females lay two eggs each.

The plated lizards, *Gerrhosaurus*, consist of six bulky species with small limbs, a long, thick tail, and a distinct fold along the flanks. They prefer grassland and live in holes at the base of shrubs, or they may live under or between rocks. They are slow-moving lizards that eat insects and mollusks, and some of the larger species also eat plant material, including berries. A seventh species, sometimes included in the genus but more often dealt with separately, is the interesting desert plated lizard, *Angolosaurus skoogi* from the Namib Desert. This lizard lives among sand dunes and has a number of unique adaptations. Its snout is wedge shaped, and its body is cylindrical, so it superficially resembles the North African sandfish, *Scincus scincus*. It is white or cream in color with scattered orange flecks, and the underside of its chin and

The Isolation Factor

Why are there so many similar species of girdle-tailed, flat, and crag lizards? The answer lies in their habitat preference—rocks. Rock outcrops, known as *koppjes* in the region, are a characteristic feature of the southern African landscape, and each will have a colony of rock-loving lizards. Many species are unique to small areas, isolated on their own particular *koppje* or groups of *koppjes,* which are surrounded by unsuitable sand or gravel flats.

So how did they get to the various outcrops in the first place? At one time, when bedrock covered the surface of the continent, the ancestors of these lizards were widespread, and their distribution was continuous. During the Pliocene and Pleistocene epochs (from about 5 to 1 million years ago), however, erosion created rivers that collected sand and silt, including the sands that later formed the Kalahari Desert. When the rivers disappeared, all the silt settled in the low-lying areas between peaks, isolating them just as if they were surrounded by ocean. The lizard colonies became cut off one by one; and with no gene flow between them, they were free to evolve independently of each other.

⊖ *The preferred habitat of the giant plated lizard,* Gerrhosaurus validus, *is the upper slopes of granite outcrops. This giant plated lizard is basking on rocks in Zimbabwe.*

chest are jet black. It feeds on beetles and dry grasses and seeds. When disturbed, it often dives into the sand and can remain buried for up to 24 hours.

The seps, or plated snake lizards, *Tetradactylus*, show a tendency to lose their limbs. There are six species. Some have small but fully formed limbs, while others have no front limbs at all and small, spinelike hind limbs. There are also intermediate forms. Their scales have keels and are arranged in longitudinal rows, so the whole body has a ridged appearance. Their tail is up to three times the length of the head and body combined. They swim through grass using it to push themselves along, closely paralleling the grass lizards, *Chamaesaura* (Cordylidae), and *Takydromus* (Lacertidae). They also use the tail to spring off the ground if they are alarmed.

The two remaining genera, *Tracheloptychus* and *Zonosaurus*, are Madagascan, with two and 16 species respectively. *Tracheloptychus petersi* has a pointed snout that it uses to force itself through sandy ground, but otherwise the habits of these two southern species are poorly known. The other species, *T. madagascariensis*, also lives in dry, sandy habitats but is not as specialized.

The *Zonosaurus* species are a little skinklike. Several, such as *Z. laticaudatus*, have prominent light-colored stripes running down the body, and they often bask at the edges of thick undergrowth in dry forest, open grassland, or forest clearings. The largest species, *Z. maximus*, grows to 27 inches (70 cm) in total length and lives along rivers and streams. Its tail is flattened from side to side, and it will often enter water when disturbed. For this reason local Malagasy people call it *petit caiman*.

LIZARDS

Black Girdle-Tailed Lizard

Cordylus niger

The elegant black girdle-tailed lizards look as though they are carved from solid jet or coal as they sit motionless, soaking up the warmth of the sun.

Common name Black girdle-tailed lizard

Scientific name *Cordylus niger*

Family Cordylidae

Suborder Sauria

Order Squamata

Size 6 in (15 cm) long

Key features Body flattened, head flat and triangular and covered with smooth shields; scales around the back of the head are smooth and do not end in spines; scales on the back are only slightly keeled but more heavily keeled along the centerline; tail spiny; both sexes as well as juveniles are completely black in color and only slightly paler beneath

Habits Diurnal and rock dwelling (saxicolous)

Breeding Live-bearer; female has litter of 1–3 large young

Diet Insects and spiders

Habitat Rock outcrops in the coastal scrub known as fynbos

Distribution South Africa; occurs only in a small area consisting of the Cape Peninsula and on coastal rocks farther north

Status Common in suitable habitat but with a limited range; protected (CITES Appendix II)

Similar species The only other black species in the same area is Oelofsen's girdle-tailed lizard, *C. oelofseni*, but dark or black species live elsewhere, especially in coastal regions

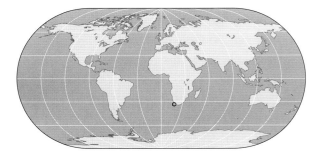

UNLIKE SOME OTHER MEMBERS of the genus, black girdle-tailed lizards lead solitary lives, emerging to bask when the sun has begun to warm up the rocks where they live. They come out slowly at first, warming just the head. Gradually they venture out completely and often choose a prominent rock on which to perch. Some of the places in which they live, such as the Cape of Good Hope Nature Reserve, have many human visitors, and lizards living near paths and picnic sites become so accustomed to people that they remain in place even if they are approached closely.

Black for Warmth

Being black helps the lizards absorb heat efficiently and quickly. Although the places where they live are often hot, that was not always the case. About 10 million years ago the region was partly covered in ice, and scientists think that the black forms of girdle-tailed lizards evolved then. With a limited amount of sunshine they needed to improve their heat absorption. One way of doing this was to increase the black pigment in their skin.

Later the climate warmed up again, and other forms of lizard moved back into the region. But the black girdle-tailed lizards still had an advantage in cooler places such as mountainsides and coastal areas. Their closest

relatives are another black species, Oelofsen's girdle-tailed lizard, *Cordylus oelofseni*, and a more widespread brown species, the Cape girdle-tailed lizard, *C. cordylus*. The latter lives over a large part of the southern Cape region.

Communication and Courtship

As in most girdle-tailed lizards, males and females are roughly similar in size and have the same coloration. This implies that males do not take part in visual territorial displays (unlike the wall lizards, iguanids, and agamids). Instead, these lizards appear to communicate with each other by chemical means. Both sexes have glands opening through a row of femoral pores on their thighs. (Lizards in some other families have similar structures, but they are rarely as conspicuous as they are in girdle-tails.) They are thought to use secretions from

⊕ *The black girdle-tailed lizard has smooth shiny scales that are only slightly keeled. It is restricted to a small area of South Africa.*

these glands to signal their sex, age, and status, and to mark the boundaries of their territory.

Little is known of courtship and mating, but females give birth to litters of one to three relatively large young in January or February. Unlike in other species, there does not seem to be a close attachment between the adult female and her young, and the juveniles are rarely seen. They probably have many predators, including snakes and birds of prey. If they survive predation, however, they are long-lived; closely related forms have survived for 15 years or more in captivity.

All *Cordylus* species are protected and placed in CITES Appendix II. They are vulnerable not because they are especially rare but because several have limited ranges. In addition, they are slow to reproduce, and populations could easily be depleted if collecting on a large scale was allowed. This is because unscrupulous collectors can destroy the lizards' habitat by prying away large rock flakes to capture them.

Other Black Girdle-Tails

Apart from *Cordylus niger* there are several other dark or black girdle-tailed lizards in South Africa. Oelofsen's girdle-tail, *C. oelofseni*, also lives in the Cape region, but has an even more restricted range. It was described in 1990. Peer's girdle-tailed lizard, *C. peersi*, lives farther north in Namaqualand, and the blue-spotted girdle-tailed lizard, *C. coeruleopunctata*, lives on rock outcrops in another small area farther east along the south coast. All of them are thought to be relics from a time when the climate was far colder.

Common name Armadillo lizard

Scientific name *Cordylus cataphractus*

Family Cordylidae

Suborder Sauria

Order Squamata

Size 7 in (18 cm) long; males are slightly larger than females

Key features Body flattened; head flat, wide, and triangular, fringed with backward-pointing spiny scales; scales on the back are very large, with only 15–17 rows between the neck and the base of the tail; each scale is keeled and ends in a small spine; tail is ringed with large spiny scales; back is pale brown with no markings; underside of the throat and body are yellowish

Habits Diurnal and rock dwelling (saxicolous)

Breeding Live-bearer; female has litter of 1 or 2 young

Diet Insects

Habitat Rocky places

Distribution Southwest South Africa

Status Becoming rare

Similar species Other girdle-tailed lizards usually have smaller scales on their back, although confusion is possible with other brown species, such as the Namaqua girdle-tailed lizard, *Cordylus namaquensis*, especially at a distance

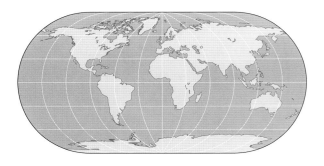

Armadillo Lizard

Cordylus cataphractus

The armadillo lizard makes good use of its heavily armored, spiny dorsal scales. When it is in danger, it bites the tip of its tail and forms itself into a loop, with its spiny scales sticking out.

LIKE THE MAMMAL AFTER WHICH IT IS NAMED, the armadillo lizard protects its more vulnerable underside from danger by curling into a loop and biting the tip of its tail. Its scientific name means "clad in armor." Its more usual form of defense, however, is to retreat into cracks in the rocks. It rarely strays far from the rocks and is extremely wary, making it difficult to approach.

Like other girdle-tailed lizards, the armadillo lizard lives in colonies centered around a rock outcrop in the dry semidesert region of southern Africa known as Namaqualand. The habitat here is succulent karoo, a landscape of low sandstone outcrops, or *koppjes*, surrounded by gravelly plains. In the south it is covered with a wealth of spectacular flowers during the short spring. Millions of insects are attracted to the flowers and provide the starting point for a food chain that includes the armadillo lizard and related species.

Armadillo lizards are sit-and-wait predators that set up an ambush station a few inches from the crevices in which they live, usually near ground level. They are slow-moving lizards and are easily captured if they are found out in the open, which is probably why their unusual defensive behavior has evolved.

Sociable Lizards

Armadillo lizards are highly sociable. Family groups stay together, so that lizards of varying ages live in the same rock crack. Groups of up to 40 lizards sometimes occur, but a group of two to six is more usual. The difference in group size seems to be related to the type and size of crack in which they live: Large groups

ⓘ *By coiling into a loop with its tail held firmly in its mouth, the armadillo lizard presents its spiny scales to an attacker and becomes almost impossible to swallow.*

live in large, inaccessible cracks, while smaller groups live in narrower crevices formed by smaller rocks. Single lizards are usually lone males, and small groups of two to four consist of a male and a female, sometimes with young.

In late summer females give birth to one or (rarely) two young, each measuring about half the length of an adult. Each young lizard weighs roughly the same as the combined weight of two to five young of other *Cordylus* species. The female therefore invests more reproductive effort into each baby than other lizards do and can also take better care of them. It is thought that this is how group living evolved. The young stay with their mother at least for the first few months of their lives, and there is some evidence that the mother may feed them, catching small insects and offering them to her offspring by mouth.

Individuals sometimes leave groups, presumably to set up home elsewhere. In recent studies scientists found that adult males and females are equally likely to move away from their group, but that juveniles are more likely to move than adults. This movement of individuals may help the lizards avoid inbreeding. In fact, when the results were analyzed, it appeared that groups were made up not of close "families" but of mixed individuals, some of which were related but many of which were not.

It is likely that the factors that control lizards' movements between one group and another are connected more to the distance between cracks than to whether or not they are related. The tail-biting behavior may have evolved because the lizards need to venture out into the open when moving between groups. If they stayed close to their crevices, the behavior of rolling into a loop may never have been necessary.

Common name Broadley's
flat lizard

Scientific name *Platysaurus broadleyi*

Family Cordylidae

Suborder Sauria

Order Squamata

Size 6 in (15 cm) long

Key features Head and body are wafer thin; back is
covered with fine, granular scales, but the
head has large platelike scales; males are
spectacular with blue head, greenish back,
and orange or yellow front legs; throat and
chest in males is electric blue, and the belly
is glossy black; females and juveniles are
brown with 3 wide cream stripes running
down the back

Habits Diurnal and rock dwelling (saxicolous)

Breeding Egg layer; female lays 2 elongated eggs in
rock crevices

Diet Mainly insects, especially flies, but also some
plant material

Habitat Granite rock outcrops

Distribution Limited to the area around the lower
Orange River in the vicinity of Augrabies Falls,
South Africa

Status Very numerous over a small area

Similar species All flat lizards are similar, but the
markings of males vary slightly; their ranges
do not overlap, so they are easily identified
by locality

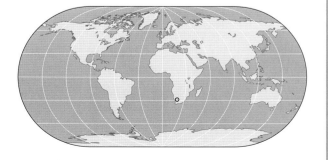

Broadley's Flat Lizard

Platysaurus broadleyi

Looking for all the world like the victims of a nasty accident, flat lizards are highly specialized rock dwellers that squeeze into the narrow crevices between granite boulders.

FLAT LIZARDS ARE WELL NAMED. They fit snugly into the tiny gaps between boulders and under flakes and caprocks. Large numbers often congregate together in a single crack, although males are territorial in the breeding season and will not share their crack with other males.

Unlike the girdle-tailed lizards, the flat lizards are highly dimorphic: Males are brightly colored, but the females and juveniles are camouflaged. Males use their colors to display to rival males as well as to females. If two males come into conflict, they circle each other, tilting their bodies by straightening the pair of legs nearest their rival. This shows off their bright blue throat and chest. After a bout of posturing the dominant male chases away the intruder. Observers have noticed that males are less likely to fight other males that have neighboring territories than males from farther afield. Presumably they reach an uneasy alliance and regard each other as less of a threat than strange males from outside the area.

Colorful Displays

The purpose of territories, of course, is to gain access to as many females as possible. Given a choice, males prefer to mate with larger females because they lay larger eggs that are more likely to produce strong hatchlings. When displaying to potential mates, male flat lizards face them head-on and raise the front half of their body to show off their colorful throat and chest.

A few weeks after mating, the females lay a pair of elongated, soft-shelled eggs. This is very unusual among cordylids, since the rest of the family are live-bearers. The female places

the eggs deep in a crevice that has filled with leaf litter or soil and retains some moisture. Several females may choose the same crevice—batches of up to 30 eggs have been discovered.

Food and Feeding

Broadley's flat lizard is insectivorous; in the summer it feasts on the billions of small black flies that swarm around the edges of the river and waterfall, even leaping into the air to catch them. The lizards go about their business of decimating the flies oblivious to large numbers of tourists that visit the Augrabies Falls. They will also eat flowers, leaves, and fruit; and later in the season they may switch to eating the fruits of the Namaqua fig, *Ficus cordata*, that grows in the region, congregating under the trees to reach the fallen berries.

⬅ *Male flat lizards in the genus* Platysaurus *are more brightly colored than the females. The vivid colors are put to good use when chasing off rival males or displaying to females.*

Why Eggs?

The flat lizards lay small clutches of eggs because in order to survive, they must be able to slip into narrow crevices. If their bodies had to accommodate developing young or larger clutches or eggs, they would not be able to do so. They would also be vulnerable to predators, the most important of which is the rock kestrel, *Falco tinnunculus*. Natural selection has therefore favored females that lay small clutches of eggs. Even though elongated, the eggs can still contain a good amount of material, so the young hatch at a relatively large size without causing the female's body to become too rounded.

In eastern Brazil an iguanid species, the striped lava lizard, *Tropidurus semitaeniatus*, does exactly the same thing. It also lives in granite outcrops and shelters in crevices. Its clutch size is two, and its eggs are elongated. On the other hand, the granite night lizard, *Xantusia henshawi* from southern California and northern Mexico, has a similar lifestyle and is flattened in the same way, but it is a live-bearer. The female gives birth to one or two young.

Cape Crag Lizard

Pseudocordylus microlepidotus

Common name Cape crag lizard

Scientific name *Pseudocordylus microlepidotus*

Family Cordylidae

Suborder Sauria

Order Squamata

Size 10 in (25 cm) long

Key features A large crag lizard with a large head and bulges on its cheeks due to its powerful jaw muscles; the scales on the back are smaller than those of girdle-tailed lizards but still arranged in regular rows; each large scale is surrounded by a number of small granular scales; limbs are well developed; tail is ringed with spiny scales; males have reddish-brown back with yellow or orange crossbars; flanks and underside of body and limbs are also yellow or orange in males

Habits Diurnal and rock dwelling (saxicolous)

Breeding Live-bearer; female has litter of 3–7 young

Diet Large grasshoppers, crickets, and beetles; occasionally small lizards

Habitat Rocky, vegetated hills and mountainsides

Distribution Southern parts of South Africa on inland mountain ranges

Status Common

Similar species The graceful crag lizard, *P. capensis*, lives in part of the range, but it is smaller, more dainty, and lives on steeper rock faces

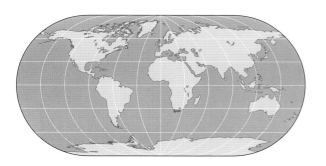

The Cape crag lizard is one of the largest members of its genus and is a powerful and aggressive species.

THE CAPE CRAG LIZARD LIVES AMONG the rocks of higher mountain slopes and excavates a chamber in large crevices by digging out the soil. This becomes its home retreat. It leads a solitary life, unlike many other rock-dwelling cordylids in which several individuals may share the same crevice. It emerges from its retreat once the sun has warmed up the surrounding rocks and moves to a prominent position from which it can watch for prey and predators. Males are often conspicuous from a distance due to their size, color, and choice of lookouts.

It is a sit-and-wait predator, making short dashes to catch prey before returning to its rock to continue surveying its territory. It feeds mainly on the large, well-armored beetles, grasshoppers, and crickets that are common in the region, and can easily crush their tough exoskeletons with its powerful jaws. Given the chance, it will also take smaller lizards.

The Cape crag lizard's main enemies come from above in the form of birds of prey, and it repeatedly scans the skies while it is basking—even captives frequently twist their head around and look up. Their most effective means of escape is to dash back into their crevice, which they do at the slightest disturbance.

Jaw Clenching

Once there, they use the jaws to wedge themselves tightly in. An unusual hinged arrangement to the skull causes it to become deeper if the jaws are clenched together. By clamping its jaws shut, the lizard forces the top of its skull upward, jamming it against the roof of the narrow crevice. The scales on top of the head are reinforced with bony plates

⊛ *As its name suggests, the Cape crag lizard is a rock dweller. It has developed an unusual way of wedging itself in narrow crevices by extending the top of its reinforced skull.*

(osteoderms) to prevent damage to the skull. It is almost impossible to dislodge the lizard when it is bracing itself against the rock in this way. At the same time, it curls its spiky tail around in front of its body, protecting its flanks.

Crag lizards do not have osteoderms under their body scales, probably to allow the body more flexibility and make it easier to squeeze into cracks. The flat lizards do not have them either, for the same reason, but the girdle-tailed lizards do. Their strategy is a little different: They jam themselves in using the backward-pointing spines on their scales like barbs.

Cape crag lizards hibernate in winter, which can be severe on the mountain slopes. At this time they tolerate each other and may hibernate communally. Courtship and breeding take place in the spring. The females give birth to between three and seven young. The young

The Relatives

The seven species of crag lizards all occur in South Africa, and their collective range describes an arc just inland from the coast, following the line of the old mountain escarpment of southern Africa. They are all rather similar in appearance and lifestyle. But one species, the dwarf crag lizard, *Pseudocordylus nebulosus*, is smaller than the others and has a slimmer body with longer limbs and tail. It comes from a single location in the Hottentots-Holland Mountains just northeast of Cape Town in an area that is characteristically moist, misty, and cool. Like the black girdle-tailed lizard, *Cordylus niger*, and similar species that come from cooler environments, this crag lizard is black in color, although it sometimes has two rows of yellow spots along the center of its back.

lizards tend to keep away from the territories of adults (perhaps because they might be eaten) and live on the edges of the scattered colonies, often on the lower slopes. As they grow, they gradually move up the slope to more prominent positions, where they make permanent homes.

Common name Giant plated
lizard

Scientific name *Gerrhosaurus validus*

Family Gerrhosauridae

Suborder Sauria

Order Squamata

Size 14 in (36 cm) long

Key features A large lizard with a flattened body and
head; tail long, often thickened at the base;
legs well developed but short; body scales
rectangular and arranged in regular rows; an
obvious fold present down each side of the
body; adults are dark brown, but each scale
on the head and back has a small yellow
spot, creating a speckled appearance; some
have a pair of cream stripes on the back;
juveniles are dark brown with larger yellow
spots on their back and crossbars on
their flanks

Habits Diurnal and terrestrial

Breeding Female lays clutch of 2–5 eggs in rock crevice

Diet Invertebrates, small vertebrates, and some
vegetable material

Habitat Grassland, mainly on rocky slopes or well-
vegetated rock outcrops

Distribution Eastern subspecies, *G. v. validus*, occurs
from northeast South Africa through
Zimbabwe and Mozambique to Malawi and
Zambia; western subspecies, *G. v. maltzahni*,
lives in Namibia

Status Common in suitable habitat

Similar species The rough-scaled plated lizard,
Gerrhosaurus major, is the other large
species, but it has heavily keeled scales and is
pale brown in color, sometimes with a stripe
down either side of its back

Giant Plated Lizard

Gerrhosaurus validus

*The largest member of its genus, the giant plated
lizard is shy and difficult to approach. When disturbed,
it squeezes itself into a crevice and inflates its body.*

THE GIANT PLATED LIZARD is large and bulky. It is
heavily armored with rows of scales and
underlying bony plates (osteoderms). Its body is
roughly cylindrical in cross-section, and its
limbs, although fully formed, are relatively
small. It is not swift or agile, and it relies on its
armor plating for defense.

The lizard usually makes a burrow between
two slabs of rocks by digging out accumulated
soil or leaf litter and never strays far from
this retreat. If it is chased into its crack, it will
inflate its body, making it difficult to dislodge. It
usually looks for food in the immediate vicinity,
using its front feet to scrape away soil at the
bases of bushes or around rocks. Its main
source of food is insects, but it also takes some
vegetable material such as flowers, fruit, and
berries. Small lizards and even baby tortoises
are also eaten. It is truly an omnivorous lizard.

Living and Breeding

Giant plated lizards inhabit dry, grassy hillsides
with rock piles or the upper slopes of vegetated
koppjes (rock outcrops). They live in loose
colonies, but they are not especially sociable.
The sexes look the same, although males often
have better-developed pores on the undersides
of the thighs. In the breeding season their chin,
throat, and sides of the head become tinged
with purple. Nothing is known of their
courtship or mating behavior. Females lay two
to five (usually four) large oval eggs in soil-filled
rock crevices in midsummer (November to
December). The hatchlings appear at the end of
summer and measure just over 6 inches (15 cm)
in total length.

When basking, plated lizards often raise
their limbs but keep their underside in contact

⊖ *Detail of the giant
plated lizard, showing
the regular scales,
flattened head, and dirty-
white throat.*

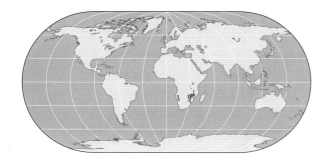

SEE ALSO Girdle-Tailed and Plated Lizards **45**:98

The Relatives

There are five other species of plated lizards. The rough-scaled plated lizard, *Gerrhosaurus major,* is also a large species. It is likely to be found in grasslands, but it hides in rock crevices and occasionally old termite mounds. It is usually light brown in color; specimens from the southern part of Africa often have dark centers to their scales and can also have a pale stripe down each side of the body, but those from the drier northern latitudes are often uniform brown. Like the giant plated lizard, this species is omnivorous. The Kalahari plated lizard, *G. multilineatus,* is similar, but its scales have light centers and darker edges, giving an overall checkered appearance. It lives in burrows beneath shrubs in the sandy soil of the Kalahari Desert.

The other three species are smaller. The yellow-throated plated lizard, *G. flavigularis*, is a handsome species. Its body is a rich brown color with a wide, bright-yellow stripe down each side of the back. The male's cheeks and throat are usually orange or yellow, becoming brighter in the breeding season, but males from some areas have blue throats. The black-lined plated lizard, *G. nigrolineatus*, is rather similar but larger and not nearly as graceful. The Namaqua plated lizard, *G. typicus*, is the smallest species at about 8 inches (20 cm) long. It is buff with dark speckling on its back and light spots on its flanks. The undersides of males turn bright orange-red in the breeding season. This is the rarest species as well as the one with the smallest range.

with the ground. They sometimes do this when moving down gentle slopes, sliding on their smooth belly scales. This is an intermediate step toward limb reduction and gives us a clue as to how limblessness may have evolved in the related seps lizards, *Tetradactylus* species.

⊖ *The giant plated lizard's favored habitat is rocky, open grassland. Like other members of its family, it uses the cracks and crevices between the rocks to hide, and its body and head are suitably flattened.*

Glossary

Words in SMALL CAPITALS refer to other entries in the glossary.

Acrodont (teeth) teeth attached to the upper edge of the jaw, as opposed to the inside surface (PLEURODONT) or in sockets (THECODONT)

Adaptation a characteristic shape, behavior, or physiological process that equips an organism (or group of related organisms) for its way of life and habitat

Advanced relatively recently evolved (opposite of "primitive")

Albino an animal that has no color pigment in its body and has red eyes

Amniotic egg an egg with a fluid-filled sac within a membrane that encloses the embryo of reptiles, birds, and mammals. Animals that produce amniotic eggs are known as amniotes

Amplexus the position adopted during mating in most frogs and many salamanders, in which the male clasps the female with one or both pairs of limbs. See AXILLARY AMPLEXUS and INGUINAL AMPLEXUS

Annuli the growth rings often visible on the shell of CHELONIANS

Anterior the front part or head and shoulders of an animal

Aposematic coloration bright coloration serving to warn a potential predator that an animal is distasteful or poisonous

Arboreal living in trees or shrubs

Autotomy self-amputation of part of the body. Some lizards practice CAUDAL autotomy: They discard all or part of their tail

Axillary amplexus mating position in frogs in which the male grasps the female behind her front limbs. See INGUINAL AMPLEXUS

Barbel a small, elongated "feeler," or sensory process, on the head, usually of aquatic animals, e.g., some pipid frogs

Binocular vision the ability to focus both eyes on a single subject. The eyes must point forward (not sideways as in most reptiles and amphibians). Binocular vision enables animals, including humans, to judge distances

Bridges the sides of a turtle's shell, attaching to the CARAPACE above and the PLASTRON below

Brille the transparent covering over the eyes of snakes and some lizards, such as geckos

Bromeliad member of a family of plants restricted to the New World. Many live attached to trees, including "urn plants" in which ARBOREAL frogs sometimes breed

Calcareous containing calcium carbonate

Carapace the upper part of the shell of turtles and tortoises, the other parts being the PLASTRON and the BRIDGES. Also used to describe the hard structure covering part of any animal's body

Caudal relating to the tail, as in subcaudal scales beneath a snake's tail and caudal (tail) fin

Chelonian a member of the ORDER Chelonia, containing all reptiles variously known as terrapins, turtles, and tortoises

Chromatophore a specialized cell containing pigment, usually located in the outer layers of the skin

Chromosome a thread-shaped structure consisting largely of genetic material (DNA), found in the nucleus of cells

Cirrus (pl. cirri) a slender, usually flexible appendage on an animal

CITES an international conservation organization: Convention on International Trade in Endangered Species

Class a TAXONOMIC category ranking below PHYLUM, containing a number of ORDERS

Cloaca the common chamber into which the urinary, digestive, and reproductive systems discharge their contents, and which opens to the exterior; from Latin meaning "sewer" or "drain"

Clutch the eggs laid by a female at one time

Continuous breeder an animal that may breed at any time of year

Convergent evolution the effect of unrelated animals looking like each other because they have adapted to similar conditions in similar ways

Coprophagy the practice of eating excrement

Costal relating to the ribs

Costal grooves grooves or folds along the flanks of caecilians and some salamanders that correspond to the position of the ribs

Crocodilian a member of the order Crocodylia, including alligators, caimans, crocodiles, and gharials

Cryptic having the ability to remain hidden, usually by means of camouflage, e.g., cryptic coloration

Cutaneous respiration breathing that takes place across the skin's surface, especially important in amphibians

Cycloid disklike, resembling a circle

Denticle toothlike scale

Dermis layer of skin immediately below the EPIDERMIS

Dewlap flap or fold of skin under an animal's throat. Sometimes used in displays, e.g., in anole lizards

Dimorphism the existence of two distinct forms within a SPECIES, which is then said to be dimorphic. In species in which there are more than two forms, they are polymorphic. See SEXUAL DIMORPHISM

Direct development transition from egg to the adult form in amphibians without passing through a free-living LARVAL stage

Dorsal relating to the back or upper surface of the body or one of its parts

Ectotherm (adj. ectothermic) an animal that relies on external heat sources, such as the sun, to raise its body temperature. Reptiles and amphibians are ectotherms. See ENDOTHERM

Eft juvenile, TERRESTRIAL phase in the life cycle of a newt. The red eft is the terrestrial juvenile form of the eastern newt, *Notophthalmus viridescens*

Egg tooth small toothlike scale that some amphibians and reptiles have on the tip of the snout to assist in breaking through their eggshell

Endemic SPECIES, GENERA, or FAMILIES that are restricted to a particular geographical region

Endotherm (adj. endothermic) an animal that can sustain a high body temperature by means of heat generated within the body by the metabolism. See ECTOTHERM

Epidermis surface layer of the skin of a vertebrate

Epiphyte plant growing on another plant but not a parasite. Includes many orchids and BROMELIADS and some mosses and ferns

Estivation a state of inactivity during prolonged periods of drought or high temperature. During estivation the animal often buries itself in soil or mud. See HIBERNATION

Estuarine living in the lower part of a river (estuary) where fresh water meets and mixes with seawater

Explosive breeder a SPECIES in which the breeding season is very short, resulting in large numbers of animals mating at the same time

External fertilization fusing of eggs and sperm outside the female's body, as in nearly all frogs and toads. See INTERNAL FERTILIZATION

Family TAXONOMIC category ranking below ORDER, containing GENERA that are more closely related to one another than any other grouping of genera

Farming hatching and rearing of young CHELONIANS and CROCODILIANS from a captive-breeding population. See RANCHING

Fauna the animal life of a locality or region

Femoral gland gland situated on an animal's thigh

Femoral pores row of pores along an animal's thighs. Most obvious in many lizards

Fertilization union of an egg and a sperm

Gamete OVUM or sperm

Genus (pl. genera) taxonomic category ranking below FAMILY; a group of SPECIES all more closely related to one another than to any other group of species

Gestation carrying the developing young within the body. Gestation period is the length of time that this occurs

Gill respiratory structure in aquatic animals through which gas exchange takes place

Gill slits slits in which GILLS are situated and present in some amphibians and their LARVAE

Granular (scale) small grainlike scales covering the body, as in some geckos and in the file snakes, *Acrochordus*

Gravid carrying eggs or young

Gular pouch area of expandable skin in the throat region

Hedonic glands glands in a male salamander that stimulate a female when they are rubbed against her body

Heliotherm an animal that basks to regulate body temperature

Hemipenis (pl. hemipenes) one of two grooved copulatory structures present in the males of some reptiles

Herbivore animal that eats plants

Heterogeneous (scales) scales that differ in shape or size. See HOMOGENEOUS (SCALES)

Hibernation a period of inactivity, often spent underground, to avoid extremes of cold. See ESTIVATION

Hinge a means by which the PLASTRON of some CHELONIANS can be pulled up, giving the reptile more protection against a would-be predator

Home range an area in which an animal lives except for MIGRATIONS or rare excursions

Homogeneous (scales) scales that are all the same shape and size. See HETEROGENEOUS (SCALES)

Hyoid "u"-shaped bone at the base of the tongue to which the larynx is attached

Inguinal pertaining to the groin

Inguinal amplexus a mating position in which a male frog or salamander clasps a female around the lower abdomen. See AXILLARY AMPLEXUS

Intergular scute a single plate, or SCUTE, lying between the paired gular scutes on the PLASTRON of side-necked turtles

Internal fertilization fusing of eggs and sperm inside the female's body, as in reptiles and most salamanders. See EXTERNAL FERTILIZATION

Interstitial the thin skin between the scales of reptiles. Sometimes called "interscalar" skin

Introduced species brought from lands where it occurs naturally to lands where it has not previously occurred

IUCN International Union for the Conservation of Nature, responsible for assigning animals and plants to internationally agreed categories of rarity. *See* table below

Jacobson's organ (or vomeronasal organ) one of a pair of grooves extending from the nasal cavity and opening into the mouth cavity in some mammals and reptiles. Molecules collected on the tongue are sampled by this organ, which supplements the sense of smell

Juvenile young animal, not sexually mature

Karst a porous form of limestone

Keeled scales a ridge on the DORSAL scales of some snakes

Keratophagy the practice of eating molted skin

Lamella (pl. lamellae) thin transverse plates across the undersides of the toes of some lizards, especially geckos

Larva (pl. larvae) early stage in the development of an animal (including amphibians) after hatching from the egg

Lateral line organ sense organ embedded in the skin of some aquatic animals, including LARVAL salamanders and some frogs, which responds to waterborne vibrations. Usually arranged in a row along the animal's side

Leucistic an animal that lacks all pigment except that in its eyes. Partially leucistic animals have patches of white over an otherwise normally pigmented skin. See ALBINO

Life cycle complete life history of an organism from one stage to the recurrence of that stage, e.g., egg to egg

Life history history of a single individual organism from the fertilization of the egg until its death

Lifestyle general mode of life of an animal, e.g., NOCTURNAL predator, aquatic HERBIVORE, parasite

Live-bearing giving birth to young that have developed beyond the egg stage. Live-bearers may be VIVIPAROUS or OVOVIVIPAROUS

Lure (noun) part of the body, such as the tail, that is used to entice prey closer

Mental gland gland on the chin of some newts and salamanders that appears to stimulate the female during courtship; one of the HEDONIC GLANDS

Metabolism chemical or energy changes occurring within a living organism that are involved in various life activities

Metamorphosis transformation of an animal from one stage of its life history to another, e.g., from LARVA to adult

Microenvironment local conditions that immediately surround an organism

Migration movement of animals from one place to another, often in large numbers and often for breeding purposes

Mimic an animal that resembles an animal belonging to another SPECIES, usually a distasteful or venomous one, or some inedible object

Milt sperm-containing fluid produced by a male frog during egg laying to fertilize the eggs

Montane pertaining to mountains or SPECIES that live in mountains

Morph form or phase of an animal

Morphological relating to the form and structure of an organism

Nasolabial groove a groove running from the nostril to the upper lip in male plethodontid salamanders

Neonate the newborn young of a live-bearer

Neoteny condition in which a LARVA fails to METAMORPHOSE and retains its larval features as an adult. Species with this condition are said to be neotenic. The axolotl is the best-known example. See PEDOMORPHOSIS

Neotropics the tropical part of the New World, including northern South America, Central America, part of Mexico, and the West Indies

Newt amphibious salamanders of the genera *Triturus, Taricha,* and *Notophthalmus*

Niche the role played by a SPECIES in its particular community. It is determined by its food and temperature preferences; each species' niche within a community is unique

Nocturnal active at night

Nuptial pad an area of dark, rough skin that develops in male amphibians on the hands, arms, or chest of some SPECIES prior to the breeding season. Its purpose is to allow the male to grip the female in AMPLEXUS

Occipital lobe the pyramid-shaped area at the back of the brain that helps an animal interpret vision

Ocular of the eye

Olfactory relating to the sense of smell

Omnivore an animal that eats both animal and plant material

Order taxonomic category ranking below CLASS and above FAMILY

Osteoderm small bone in the skin of some reptiles; lies under the scales

Ovary female gonad or reproductive organ that produces the OVUM

Overwinter survive the winter

Oviduct the duct in females that carries the OVUM from the ovary to the CLOACA

Oviparous reproducing by eggs that hatch outside the female's body

IUCN CATEGORIES

EX	**Extinct,** when there is no reasonable doubt that the last individual of the species has died.		**VU**	**Vulnerable,** when a species is facing a high risk of extinction in the wild in the medium-term future.
EW	**Extinct in the Wild,** when a species is known only to survive in captivity or as a naturalized population well outside the past range.		**LR**	**Lower Risk,** when a species has been evaluated and does not satisfy the criteria for CR, EN, or VU.
			DD	**Data Deficient**, when there is not enough information about a species to assess the risk of extinction.
CR	**Critically Endangered,** when a species is facing an extremely high risk of extinction in the wild in the immediate future.		**NE**	**Not Evaluated,** species that have not been assessed by the IUCN criteria.
EN	**Endangered,** when a species is facing a very high risk of extinction in the wild in the near future.			

Ovoviviparous reproducing by eggs that the female retains within her body until they hatch; the developing eggs contain a yolk sac but receive no nourishment from the mother through a placenta or similar structure

Ovum (pl. ova) female germ cell or GAMETE; an egg cell or egg

Papilla (pl. papillae) aised projection(s) of soft tissue often seen on the head and neck of aquatic CHELONIANS

Parietal eye a VESTIGIAL eye situated in the top of the head of tuataras and some lizards, sometimes known as the "third eye"

Parietals pairs of bones forming the rear of the roof of the brain case

Parotid glands pair of large glands on the shoulder, neck, or behind the eye in some salamanders and toads

Parthenogenesis a form of asexual reproduction in which the OVUM develops without being fertilized. Such SPECIES are said to be parthenogenetic

Parturition the process of giving birth to live young

Pectoral girdle the skeleton supporting the forelimbs of a land vertebrate

Pedogenesis form of reproduction by an animal still showing LARVAL characteristics

Pedomorphosis the retention of immature or LARVAL characteristics, such as GILLS, by animals that are sexually mature. See NEOTENY

Permeable property of a substance, such as skin, allowing another substance, such as water, to pass through it

Pheromone a substance released by an organism to induce a response in another individual of the same SPECIES, such as sexual attraction

Phylum taxonomic category ranking above CLASS and below kingdom

Pigment a substance that gives color to part or all of an organism's body

Plastron the ventral portion, or underside, of the shell of a turtle

Pleurodont teeth teeth that are attached to the inside surface of the jaw, as opposed to the upper edge (ACRODONT) or in sockets (THECODONT)

Pond-type larva salamander LARVA with high fins and a deep body, adapted to living in still water. See STREAM-TYPE LARVA

Preanal pores chemical- or pheromone-secreting pores in front of the CLOACA, usually in lizards

Prehensile adapted for grasping or clasping, especially by wrapping around, such as the tail of chameleons

Preocular relating to the front of the eye

Ranching artificial incubation of eggs collected from the wild followed by captive-rearing of the young. A method used with both CHELONIANS and CROCODILIANS to increase population numbers, carried out in an environment free from predators

Rectilinear locomotion a form of movement used by heavy-bodied snakes in which the body progresses in a straight line

Riffle agitated water flowing over rocks or gravel in shallow streams or rivers

Rostral processes extensions to the snout, including horns and other ornamentation

Salt glands glands located in the vicinity of the eye that allow marine turtles and some CROCODILIANS to excrete excessive salt from their bodies, helping prevent them from becoming dehydrated in the marine environment

Satellite male a male frog that does not call but sits near a calling male and intercepts females attracted to the calling male

Savanna open grasslands with scattered trees and bushes, usually in warm areas

Scute enlarged scale on a reptile, including the colorful scales that cover the shell of turtles; divided into different groups, such as the vertebral scutes that run above the VERTEBRAL COLUMN

Sexual dimorphism the existence of marked morphological differences between males and females

Species taxonomic category ranking below GENUS; a group of organisms with common attributes capable of interbreeding and producing healthy fertile offspring

Spermatheca a pouch or sac in the female reproductive tract in which sperm are stored

Spermatophore a structure containing sperm that is passed from the male to the female in some animals, such as in many salamanders

Stream-type larva streamlined LARVA with low fins and elongated body, adapted for living in flowing water. See POND-TYPE LARVA

Subcaudal beneath the tail, as in "subcaudal" scales. See CAUDAL

Subocular usually refers to scales below the eye. See PREOCULAR

Subspecies a locally distinct group of animals that differ slightly from the normal appearance of the SPECIES; often called a race

Substrate the solid material on which an organism lives, e.g., sand, mud, etc.

Suture the zigzag patterning formed beneath the SCUTES where the bones of a CHELONIAN's shell fuse together

Tadpole LARVAL stage of a frog or toad

Talus slopes slopes covered with loose rocks and slabs. Also known as scree

Taxonomy the science of classification: the arrangement of animals and plants into groups based on their natural relationships

Temporal relating to the area between the eye and ear

Terrestrial living on land

Territorial defending an area so as to exclude other members of the same SPECIES

Territory an area that one or more animals defends against other members of the same SPECIES

Thecodont teeth growing in sockets. See ACRODONT

Thermoregulate to expose to or move away from a heat source in order to maintain desired body temperature

Thermoregulation control of body temperature by behavioral or physiological means, so that it maintains a constant or near-constant value

Thyroid gland a gland lying in the neck that produces the hormone THYROXINE

Thyroxine a hormone containing iodine that is involved in a variety of physiological processes, including METAMORPHOSIS in amphibians

Toad any stout-bodied, warty-skinned frog, especially one living away from water. The term has no TAXONOMIC basis, although members of the FAMILY Bufonidae are often called toads

Tongue-flicking constant use of the tongue by snakes and some lizards when exploring their surroundings. Used in conjunction with JACOBSON'S ORGAN

Tubercle a small, knoblike projection

Turtle any shelled reptile, including tortoises and terrapins

Tympanum (pl. tympana) eardrum

Unisexual species a SPECIES consisting only of females, in which reproduction is by PARTHENOGENESIS

Unken reflex a defensive posture shown by some amphibians when attacked, in which the body is arched inward with the head and tail lifted upward. Its purpose is to display a brightly colored underside

Uterine milk a uterine secretion that provides developing embryos with nourishment

Vent the CLOACAL opening of the body. Measurements of reptiles and amphibians are often given as "snout-vent" lengths or simply "s-v" lengths

Ventral describing the lower surface of the body or one of its parts

Vertebral column the spinal skeleton, or backbone, consisting of a series of vertebrae extending from the skull to the tip of the tail

Vertebrate a member of the subphylum Vertebrata, comprising all animals with a VERTEBRAL COLUMN, including fish, amphibians, reptiles, birds, and mammals

Vestigial smaller and of more simple structure than in an evolutionary ancestor. In reptiles and amphibians often used to describe limbs that have become reduced in size through the evolutionary process

Viviparous giving birth to living young that develop within and are nourished by the mother. Often used incorrectly, however, to describe any live-bearing species. See also OVOVIVIPAROUS

Volar pores pores on the underside of the feet

Webbing folds of skin present between the toes of both CROCODILIANS and aquatic CHELONIANS

Xeric adapted to life in an extremely dry habitat

Yolk sac a large sac containing stored nutrients, present in the embryos of fish, amphibians, reptiles, and birds

Further Reading

General

Arnold, E. N., *A Field Guide to the Reptiles and Amphibians of Britain and Europe*, Harper Collins, London, 2002

Behler, J. L., and King, F. W., *The Audubon Society Field Guide to North American Reptiles and Amphibians*, Alfred A. Knopf, New York, 1979

Branch, W. R., *Field Guide to the Snakes and Other Reptiles of Southern Africa*, Struik, Cape Town, 1998

Cloudsley-Thompson, J. L., *The Temperature and Water Relations of Reptiles*, Merrow, London, 1971

Cogger, H. G., *Reptiles and Amphibians of Australia*, 6th edn., Reed New Holland, Sydney, 2000

Glaw, F., and Vences, M., *A Field Guide to the Reptiles and Amphibians of Madagascar*, 2nd edn., published by the authors, Bonn, 1994

Grismer, L. L., *Amphibians and Reptiles of Baja California*, University of California Press, Berkeley, CA, 2002

Halliday, T., and Adler, C. (eds.), *The New Encyclopedia of Reptiles and Amphibians*, Firefly Books, New York and Toronto/Oxford University Press, Oxford, 2002

Murphy, J. B., Adler, K., and Collins, J. T. (eds.), *Captive Management and Conservation of Reptiles and Amphibians*, Society for the Study of Amphibians and Reptiles, Ithaca, NY, 1994

Savage, J. M., *Amphibians and Reptiles of Costa Rica*, University of Chicago Press, Chicago, 2002

Schleich, H. H., Kästle, W., and Kabisch, K., *Amphibians and Reptiles of North Africa*, Koeltz Scientific Books, Koenigstien, 1996

Spawls, S., Howell, K., Drewes, R., and Ashe, J., *A Field Guide to the Reptiles of East Africa*, Academic Press, London, 2002

Zug, G. R., Vitt, L. J., and Caldwell, J. P., *Herpetology: an Introductory Biology of Reptiles and Amphibians*, 2nd edn., Academic Press, San Diego, 2001

Specific to this volume

Anderson, S. C., *The Lizards of Iran*, Society for the Study of Amphibians and Reptiles, Ithaca, NY, 1999

Henkel, F. W., and Schmidt, W., *Geckos*, Krieger Publishing Company, Malabar, FL, 1995

Pianka, E. R., *Ecology and Natural History of Desert Lizards*, Princeton University Press, Princeton, NJ, 1986

Pianka, E. R., and Vitt, L. J., *Lizards: Windows to the Evolution of Diversity*, University of California Press, Berkeley, CA, 2003

Smith, H. M., *Handbook of Lizards*, Cornell University Press, Ithaca, NY, 1995

Storr, G. M., Smith, L. A., and Johnstone, R. E., *Lizards of Western Australia*, parts 1, 2, and 3, Western Australian Museum, Perth, 1981, 1983, 1990

Useful Websites

General

Myers, P. 2001. "Vertebrata" (On-line), Animal Diversity. Accessible at:
http://animaldiversity.ummz.umich.edu/site/accounts/information/Reptilia.html

http://www.embl-heidelberg.de/~uetz/LivingReptiles.html
The University of Heidelberg reptile database. List of species with bibliographies and links to important references

http://www.herplit.com/
A listing of herpetological literature, including older material

http://www.kingsnake.com
Many pages about reptiles and amphibians, especially their care in captivity, and links to other organizations

http://www.redlist.org
IUCN Red List gives details of all threatened animals, including reptiles and amphibians

http://www.si.edu/resource/faq/nmnh/zoology.htm#vz
General information about reptiles and amphibians and links to many educational sites

http://tolweb.org/tree/
A collaborative Internet project produced by biologists from around the world, containing information about the diversity of organisms on earth, their history, and characteristics

Specific to this volume

http://www.gekkota.com/
The website of the Global Gecko Association, with photos, caresheets, and links

http://www.repticzone.com/
A website providing information on reptiles and amphibians. Includes useful links to caresheets for geckos and plated lizards

Set Index

A **bold** number shows the volume and is followed by the relevant page numbers (e.g., **21:** 52, 74).

Common names in **bold** (e.g., **adder**) mean that the animal has an illustrated main entry in the set. Underlined page numbers (e.g., **29:** 78–79) refer to the main entry for that animal.

Italic page numbers (e.g., **22:** *103*) point to illustrations of animals in parts of the set other than the main entry.

Page numbers in parentheses—e.g., **21:** (24)—locate information in At-a-Glance boxes.

Animals that have main entries in the set are indexed under their common names, alternative common names, and scientific names.

117

121

Picture Credits